WILLIAM
THE PEOPLE'S PRINCE

HIS LIFE IN PICTURES

A NUNN SYNDICATION BOOK

PUBLISHED BY HAYDEN PUBLISHING

Hayden Publishing Ltd
32 Winifred Road
Apsley
Hemel Hempstead
HP3 9DX

Copyright © 2003 by Nunn Syndication Ltd

The right of Robin Nunn to be identified as author of this work has been asserted by him in accordance with the Copyright, Designs and Patents Act 1988.

ISBN 1 903635 12 8

A CIP catalogue record for this book can be obtained from the British Library.

The publisher would like to thank Toby Melville for the pictures taken in Chile on behalf of the Royal Rota. The book would have been incomplete without them.

Designed by Nadine Levy and David Costa at Wherefore Art?
Colour origination by PDQ Digital Media Solutions Ltd, Bungay
Printed and bound in Great Britain by Butler & Tanner Ltd, Frome

www.nunn-syndication.com
www.william-thepeoplesprince.com

foreword

I am a photographer. My company, Nunn Syndication Limited, has only one purpose – to take the best photographs and have them published in the world's great newspapers and magazines. This is, therefore, primarily a book of pictures.

When we began to look closely at our archive for pictures of Prince William, we were amazed to find a library of over five thousand images, many of them still stored as negatives and transparencies. My colleague Aasta Børte brought a degree of professionalism, profound knowledge and amazing energy to the weeks of research and picture selection. Frankly, without Aasta's expert supervision there would be no company archive or book!

Thanks are also due to my colleague David Porter, lawyer Adam Tudor of Peter Carter-Ruck and partners, whose work behind the scenes has made this project viable and my publisher Jonathan Hayden, co-writer Luke Nicoli and our Production Manager Paul Hurran for actually putting the book together.

Prince William is destined, one day, to be the King of England and the United Kingdom, Sovereign Leader of the Commonwealth. He is grandson of Queen Elizabeth II and firstborn son of Charles, Prince of Wales.

He is also Diana's son.

So much has been written about the late Diana, Princess of Wales, and I certainly do not wish to add to it. However, during the fifteen years I had the honour and privilege to travel the world and photograph the world's most photographed woman, one thing was clear – she was utterly unique. She brought hope where previously there was none, she brightened even the saddest lives and I'm certain she would have made a most marvellous 21st century queen.

This book contains the work of many great photographers but a special mention has to go to Jim Bennett. His outstanding professional contribution, particularly in the early years, was invaluable.

On a personal note I must also thank Kent Gavin, Phil (The Daddy) Dampier, Robert Jobson, Mike Lloyd and Mike Dunlea for our shared global experiences over the past twenty years.

I also wish to say a special thank you to all of my detractors for all the obstacles they continually put in my way. They kept me focused throughout and has made the taste of victory and success all the sweeter. Thanks guys!

Robin Nunn
London, 2003

For Jean and John

WILLIAM
THE PEOPLE'S PRINCE

A Royal Birth

At precisely 9.03pm on 21 June 1982, bells tolled the length and breadth of Great Britain greeting the much-anticipated arrival of William Arthur Philip Louis, first child to the Prince and Princess of Wales.

As the 7lb 10oz bouncing baby boy launched into his first few wails, the birth not only delivered a new heir to the throne but, thanks to his mother's determination to give birth to, and in due course, raise her son in her own way, it would also have far-reaching implications for the British royal family's role in modern-day society. For this was a prince who would break free from much of the tradition and protocol of previous generations; he would, as Princess Diana said: "live as normal a life that is humanly possible". He would become a figurehead for the nation, a royal to be respected and adored. He would become the People's Prince.

Diana's influence on her son was immediate and the delivery arguably her statement of intent. As the fair-haired, blue-eyed boy was born in the high-tech confines of the Lindo Wing of London's St Mary's Hospital, it appeared, to the outside world, a perfectly natural arrival. Yet within royal circles, a very private tradition had been breached: William was the first future heir to the throne to be born outside the walls of Buckingham Palace since the birth of Prince Edward (the future Edward VII) in 1841.

Diana's decision had not met with approval from within the royal household, despite the young, modern mother-to-be's understandable desire to give birth with the very best in neo-natal technology on hand. And, much to the surprise of other royal mothers, Diana also made it clear that she intended to breastfeed her child. She would have Charles's blessing on both counts, but from the outset, raising their son in a manner appropriate for a future king would always be of paramount importance to both of them in their distinctly different ways.

There is a common misconception that the young Charles was out of touch with modern society – he was considered too stuffy, inward-looking and set in his ways. Yet behind the public persona existed a playful Prince who loved his regular games of polo, shooting and – probably most surprising of all – entertaining female 'guests' at Sandringham or Buckingham Palace.

He would meet Lady Diana Spencer for the first time in 1977 during a pheasant shoot at the Spencer family home at Althorp, Northamptonshire. Introduced to Charles by her elder sister Sarah, 'Shy Di' as she was affectionately known, would, over the next four years, grow increasingly close to the Prince. Following an invitation to Charles's 30th birthday dance at Buckingham Palace, it became apparent that a serious relationship was in the offing.

Born at Park House on the Sandringham estate on 1 July 1961, the Honourable Diana Frances Spencer belonged to one of England's oldest aristocratic families. Her father was the eighth Earl of Spencer and her family tree had several royal connections – in fact, she and Charles were sixteenth cousins once removed. Diana was related to Winston Churchill and, perhaps rather more surprisingly, to no fewer than eight US presidents (George Washington, John Adams, John Quincy Adams, Calvin Coolidge, Millard Fillmore, Rutherford B Hayes, Grover Cleveland and Franklin D Roosevelt). Although her family had given several hundred years of service to the Crown, Diana was not initially regarded by many as suitable princess material – after all, if she married Charles she would become the future queen.

Occupying a modest three-bedroom flat in South Kensington, which she shared with three girlfriends, and driving about town in her modest Mini, Diana contributed her share of the rent out of her earnings from her job at the Young England Kindergarten. As their trysts became more frequent, the couple became the subject of intense media scrutiny. The 'Royal Love Train' story which appeared in the *Sunday Mirror* first brought them onto the tabloid front pages. The article claimed that Diana had twice visited Charles on the royal train as it stood in sidings in Wiltshire and, in order to bring an end to the press speculation, Her Majesty the Queen instructed her press secretary to speak to Charles: if Diana was the woman he wanted, then their affections should be made common knowledge.

The royal engagement was officially announced by Buckingham Palace at 11.00am on 24 February 1981. Looking young and radiant in a blue suit, Diana faced, for the first time, the overwhelming degree of press attention that would, in time, become the bane of her life. Obviously overawed by the flashing and glaring camera lights and a phalanx of microphones from the world's media, Diana was asked whether she was looking forward to becoming Queen of England to which she answered modestly, "With Prince Charles beside me, I cannot go wrong."

The fairytale wedding at St Paul's Cathedral on 29 July 1981 would attract a television audience in excess of 750 million and was a welcome distraction for a population enduring a recession-dogged, high-unemployment, riot-torn Britain. No expense was to be spared. This lavish wedding was prefaced by 101 celebratory bonfires that were lit from John O'Groats to Land's End; the night before the ceremony saw a huge fireworks display in Hyde Park, London; and the wedding route itself was awash with regal pomp, splendour and colour provided by some 4,500 blooms.

Diana would travel to meet her prince in a glass coach wearing a sumptuous ivory silk taffeta and antique lace Emanuel dress, hand-embroidered with 10,000 finest mother-of-pearl sequins. With a congregation of 2,500 gathered beneath the celebrated dome, the ceremony went almost without a hitch. The bride's nerves showed briefly when she inverted Charles's name to Philip Charles Arthur George, and Charles also fluffed his vows, pledging "with all thy goods I share with thee".

A radiant seven-months pregnant Lady Di was greeted with warmth verging on hysteria as she and Charles went on a walkabout in Liverpool the day before the Grand National.

As the newly married couple travelled on their 22-minute journey to Buckingham Palace in the open 1902 state postillion landau, the two million people who lined the route greeted the future king and queen with warm and enthusiastic applause, wildly waving union flags and showering them with confetti and flowers. For 24 hours, the nation was all smiles.

Almost immediately, speculation began about the possibility – and indeed probability – of a royal birth. When would it happen? How many children would the couple have? Names and schools were widely debated as the press in general, and the tabloids in particular, continued to devote acres of coverage to the royal couple. It was a honeymoon period in all senses. Yet away from an adoring public, their first year of marriage would prove to be anything but a period of enduring marital bliss. Following the honeymoon at Broadlands, Hampshire (the home of Lord and Lady Romsey,) and a cruise around the Mediterranean on the royal yacht *Britannia*, it soon became apparent to those close to the couple that all was not well.

The private relationship between the newlyweds was a very different affair to the public show of affection that had been on offer to Fleet Street, and the announcement of Diana's pregnancy in November 1981 ensured that the increasing unhappiness of the marriage remained hidden. While there may well have been a lack of marital happiness within the walls of Kensington Palace – the couple's so-called 'love nest' – Charles's interest in his wife's pregnancy and welfare was unquestionably sincere.

Contrary to many reports, he was very much looking forward to becoming a father. Charles's own childhood had been governed largely by strict routine and, compared with more modern standards, a somewhat restricted and overly formal contact with his parents. By his own admission, his closest bond of trust and affection – which would in later life develop into the most supportive and intimate of his family relationships – was with his grandmother, Queen Elizabeth the Queen Mother. Reared mainly by his nanny, Mabel Anderson, Charles would spend months separated from his parents in the early years as they embarked on their relentless timetable of royal engagements, while his teenage years were spent in the austere surrounds of Gordonstoun, a boarding school in northeast Scotland.

Charles made it abundantly clear that his future child would be born into a closer, more intimate family situation and, once the pregnancy was confirmed, he became absolutely determined to mould himself into a model father. He would read a library of books on childbirth, labour and the role of modern fatherhood.

For the first time in recent royal history, and reflecting the way the nation had taken the fairytale couple to their hearts, the pregnancy became a very public affair. Not a day went by without intense media discussion of the impending royal birth. Column inches were filled with commentary on the constitutional implications of the new arrival, speculation about the sex of the child, questions about how a new young royal would find a role in society, while a clutch of writers made it their sole purpose to monitor Diana's antenatal health. Her day-to-day appearance became a national obsession.

> Almost immediately, speculation began about the possibility – and indeed probability – of a royal birth. When would it happen? How many children would the couple have?

By now there existed an unquestioned love affair between the young Princess and the British people that had begun on the wedding day and showed no signs of cooling off. Wherever she went – officially or unofficially, publicly or privately – she would always be accompanied by dozens of photographers and reporters, all desperate to record the minutiae of her life for their insatiable readers. Without warning, and with little or no preparation, Diana had been elevated to the status of a superstar; a position she would inhabit for the rest of her life and view with considerable ambivalence.

As Diana's pregnancy advanced she continued to look absolutely radiant. Eventually the baby was induced after a gruelling 17-hour labour during which, at one point, a caesarean section was contemplated. Charles remained at his wife's bedside throughout and was an excited onlooker as the baby boy was born. Although kept secret from the public, the couple had known the baby's sex for some time – a nursery decorated in yellow and blue had already been prepared, with all the cuddly bears, toys and lullaby comforters a baby could possible need.

A crude cardboard placard was hung from the gates of St Mary's Hospital in Paddington proclaiming: 'It's a boy', and two hours later Charles emerged onto the steps of the hospital to the sounds of 'For he's a jolly good fellow' as he greeted the legions of well-wishers and the assembled press. "Nearly 17 hours is a long time to wait," said the Prince as the questioning got underway. "Obviously I'm relieved, delighted ... I think it's marvellous. It's rather a grown-up thing, I've found. It's rather a shock." When asked about the Prince's hair, he replied: "It's blond, sort of fairish." A bystander in the crowd yelled: "Is he the most beautiful baby in the world?" at which Charles grinned, "He's not bad." "Is he like his dad?" asked another. "No," the Prince replied. "He's lucky enough not to be." "Give us another one, Charlie!" shouted another bystander, but the Prince shook his head and replied "You'll have to ask my wife about that." He then let his words drift for a moment before adding: "Bloody hell, give us a chance!"

But the one question the world had waited so intently for remained unanswered: the name of the young Prince. "We have a few names in mind," said

With only a few days to go before the birth of William, Charles and Diana found time to watch polo at the Guards Club.

Charles. "You'll have to ask my wife about that. There is an argument about it." There was certainly a heated debate surrounding the child's name. Diana was thought to favour more modern names such as Sebastian or Oliver, whereas Charles wanted something more traditional. It would take a week before they came to an agreement, during which time young William was known simply as 'Baby Wales'.

Within 24 hours of the birth, the proud parents left hospital for home and William, wrapped up warm in his pristine, white lace shawl, was introduced briefly to the press with just his baby button nose and eyes visible. The couple were whisked back to Kensington Palace in a waiting car to begin life as parents and face the realities of family life.

First on the agenda was the appointment of a nanny. Again, the parents had differing views on exactly who should take on such an important role; it was certainly not a decision that could or should be taken lightly. Charles had expressed a desire that his own nanny, Mabel Anderson, should be brought out of retirement whereas Diana was once again determined to break with royal tradition by bringing in an 'outsider'. She had the final choice and Barbara Barnes, the 42-year-old daughter of a retired forestry worker, was entrusted with the position. The appointment failed to win widespread approval among the royal household as Ms Barnes had no credentials or formal training. However, she had worked for Princess Margaret's friends, Lord and Lady Glenconner, as a nanny to their youngest children, twins May and Amy Tennant.

Charles agreed reluctantly to the appointment and it didn't take long for Nanny Barnes to assume a dominant role in the Kensington Palace household. Although Diana was intent on taking a pivotal role in raising her son, the new nanny would play an important part in William's early upbringing, insisting on being present whenever William went to bed or woke up. She appointed her own 'backroom team' of Olga Powell and Ann Wallace to assist through the night or whenever Diana and Charles were absent on their growing list of royal engagements.

Publicly, precious little was seen of William in his first year, his most high profile engagement being his christening by Dr Robert Runcie, the Archbishop of Canterbury, on 4 August 1982 in the Music Room at Buckingham Palace. Surrounded by his immediate family members, the service took place in the same room and he wore the same Honiton lace gown that his father and every future monarch had worn since Edward VII. William did not take kindly to the holy water and cried throughout the service.

His next public appearance would be at Christmas 1982 where, together with his parents, he posed for photographers. For once, Diana kept a low profile, holding William's favourite teething ring while father and son took centre stage, playing together blissfully. For the first time, the world had a glimpse of Charles as the doting father. His hands-on approach was proof that he was making a concerted effort to bond with his son, particularly in the first year of his life. Charles had restricted his own official engagements in that crucial first year, and

apart from a brief nine-day break with his wife in the Bahamas, made himself available to assist whenever and wherever possible.

In March 1983 the Prince and Princess of Wales undertook their first official tour together, flying to Australia and New Zealand. It was to be an arduous six-week trip and the couple's decision to take their young son with them prompted considerable public debate. At one point it was reported, quite wrongly as it turned out, that Diana was defying her mother-in law's wishes by taking William on the trip, but there were genuine concerns that the 27-hour flight and numerous internal trips would take their toll on the nine-month-old Prince. The Foreign Office had argued on more than one occasion that: "It is not possible for the baby to accompany the royal couple." But Diana made it clear that she could not and would not be parted from her son, so after careful consideration by all parties involved, and at the request of Australian Prime Minister Malcolm Fraser, it was finally decided that William would make the trip. In doing so, he became the first royal baby to embark on an overseas trip – another break with tradition.

"Diana is delighted and extremely happy that Prince William will be going with her", a member of her Kensington staff reported at the time. "She never wanted to be separated from her baby and that is a natural feeling for any mother." Precision planning was now needed to make the trip as comfortable as possible for the young Prince. In Australia and New Zealand, temperatures in March often reach 30°C and it was decided that William would not join his parents on their gruelling schedule of flights from one state capital to another for a succession of walkabouts, receptions and banquets. Instead he would remain with Nanny Barnes at Woomargama, a large stone-built country house in New South Wales, some 11,000 miles from his Kensington Palace home. The doting parents would return whenever their engagements permitted and, as things turned out, the entire trip proved to be a resounding success, even for William, who took his tentative first steps at Government House in Wellington, New Zealand, the Wales's base for the final two weeks of their excursion.

Signs of William's growing public confidence came that winter when he spoke his first words at his very own press conference. Wearing a blue winter warmer suit, emblazoned with the words ABC on the front, he said the word 'helicopter' as his mother asked the name of the small toy she was holding.

As the young Prince became more active, so he became more adventurous, exploring the endless rooms of Kensington Palace and creating the sort of havoc with which many parents of toddlers can identify! His antics earned William the nicknames 'Basher' and 'Willie Wombat', as the sound of breaking glass and china became all too frequent. His inquisitive nature would also test his grandparents' patience on his first visit to Balmoral Castle in Scotland and members of the royal household grew increasingly worried at Nanny Barnes's apparent lack of control of her charge. Certainly as far as Charles was concerned, Barnes's competence was in doubt. Discipline would be imperative to keep the

"Give us another one, Charlie!" shouted another bystander, but the Prince shook his head and replied "You'll have to ask my wife about that." He then let his words drift for a moment before adding: "Bloody hell, give us a chance!"

rampant royal at bay.

About this time, Charles embarked on many trips abroad including Brunei and East Africa, providing Diana with the time to cement the bond between mother and son. With nursery school still a year away, she devoted most of her spare time to William. It was not uncommon for the pair to pop over to Buckingham Palace for dips in the pool and William was able to swim by the age of three – an early indication perhaps of the excellent all-round athlete he would become in the future.

The family came together again as a coherent unit in June 1984 for the annual Trooping the Colour, the official ceremony that takes place in June each year to mark the Queen's birthday at Horseguard's Parade in London.

After the formal ceremony, the royal family gathered on the balcony of Buckingham Palace to watch an RAF flypast and the first signs of strain between Diana and Charles began to creep into the public consciousness. Diana, now heavily pregnant with her second child, looked decidedly glum, while Charles, absorbed by the pomp and excitement of the day, appeared to disregard his wife's obvious distress.

Later that month, William celebrated his second birthday. Having missed out on the celebrations the previous year, following their extended tour of Canada, Charles and Diana were determined to make this a day to remember for the young Prince. A specially modified, electrically powered, bright red Jaguar XJS Cabriolet sports car proved to be his favourite present and, in the coming months, would be seen regularly around the Palace grounds. Like his outdoor pursuits, cars and motorbikes would become a passion of the young Prince – even if his first legitimate vehicle was to be a rather more modest Volkswagen Golf!

His birthday seemed to bring the warring Wales's closer together, likewise the arrival of Prince Henry, or Harry as he would become affectionately known. At 4.20pm on 15 September 1984, the Princess gave birth to a 6lb 14oz boy. Although born in the same Lindo Wing of St Mary's Hospital in Paddington as his brother, the post-birth celebrations in the streets outside were muted in comparison to those that had greeted William's arrival two years earlier.

The proud parents sweep through the gates of Buckingham Palace on their way to the Music Room for William's christening by the Archbishop of Canterbury.

THE CUSTOM OF TROOPING THE COLOUR DATES BACK TO THE 18TH CENTURY OR earlier when the guards and sentries for the royal palaces and other important buildings in London were mounted daily on the parade ground by the Horseguard's building. In the past, when the colours of a regiment were used as a rallying point in battle, they were trooped slowly down the ranks so that they could be seen and recognised by the soldiers. In 1748 it was ordered that this parade would also mark the official birthday of the sovereign.

This colourful display of pageantry is now held on the occasion of the Queen's official birthday in June each year. The Queen first rode Burmese, a pure black mare, on the 1969 parade. In 1981 a young man in the crowd fired a starter pistol at the Queen just as she turned into Horseguard's Parade, startling her horse. However, seemingly unperturbed, she soon brought her horse under control and the ceremony continued as normal. Burmese was retired in 1987, from which date the Queen has attended the parade in a carriage. The scarlet tunic worn by the Queen when she rode on horseback always bore the badges and button groupings corresponding to the regiment whose colour was being trooped that year, however she no longer wears her uniforms as they were essentially designed as riding outfits.

During the ceremony at Horseguard's Parade, the Queen is greeted by a royal salute and carries out an inspection of the troops. After the musical 'troop' by the massed bands, the escorted regimental colour is carried down the ranks; the Foot Guards and the Household Cavalry then march past the Queen, and the King's Troop, Royal Horse Artillery rank past. The Queen rides back to Buckingham Palace at the head of her guards before taking the salute at the Palace from a dais.

Indicative of what was to follow, Henry Charles Albert David found himself firmly in his sibling's shadow.

As second in line to the throne, it was inevitable that William would take the lion's share of attention. The blond hair and blue eyes, so reminiscent of his mother, provided the perfect picture for the assembled media masses, whereas Harry remained somewhat in the shadows. Not that William saw his brother in that light – even at such a tender age, his compassion, another inherent feature of his mother, shone out. Immensely protective of Harry, his affection was evident from the first day and the jealousy that so often accompanies the birth of a younger

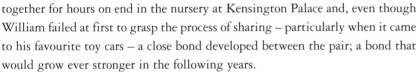

sibling simply failed to materialise.

Diana can take a great deal of credit for helping to establish a loving relationship between the brothers. She insisted that her eldest son should participate whenever possible in helping to feed, bath and change the baby. The boys played together for hours on end in the nursery at Kensington Palace and, even though William failed at first to grasp the process of sharing – particularly when it came to his favourite toy cars – a close bond developed between the pair; a bond that would grow ever stronger in the following years.

While Harry continued to grow accustomed to his new surroundings away from the media spotlight at Kensington Palace, William's public persona started to flourish as his confident, almost bullish nature came under the most intense media scrutiny. A nation looked on in fascination as the future king began to evolve from a baby to a confident, outgoing toddler. Although he shared many of his mother's characteristics, he certainly wasn't camera shy and he happily approached the assembled photographers at official press engagements – to poke and meddle with their equipment!

On one particular trip to Balmoral in 1985, the growing affinity between the press and William became particularly apparent as both parties shared a flight from London Heathrow to Aberdeen. The assembled journalists were requested to keep their distance from the young Prince, who was accompanied on the trip by Nanny Barnes and a detective. But the fact that the media was even allowed on board was a further demonstration of the open relationship that existed between the Waleses and the press at that time.

Yet even more significant on this particular trip was the fact that William was flying from London to Aberdeen without either of his parents. Although to most people it might seem strange that a three-year-old should embark on such a journey without at least one parent, royal protocol dictates that the heir to the

William is to grow very familiar with Aberdeen airport in the years to come. In 1983 he is seen arriving with Nanny Barnes on his way to Balmoral and later in the year preparing to travel back to London with Diana.

throne, in this case Charles, should not fly in the same aircraft as his successor. In the unlikely event of an air accident, two generations of the Crown would be lost. This protocol has only rarely been broken; when Charles accompanied his son from Sandringham to Aberdeen, the Queen's approval was needed and many consultations took place before she agreed to the request. The Queen has never flown in the same aircraft as Charles, and even when, many years later, William was desperate to accompany his father to bring Diana's body back from Paris, it was decided that he should remain with his brother at Balmoral.

Another tradition that played a prominent role in the life of the young Prince, but which largely stopped once Charles and Diana began to live separate lives, was the annual trip aboard the royal yacht *Britannia*. From Portsmouth, William would accompany his parents around the coast of Britain, through the Western Isles of Scotland and onto the deep-water harbour of Scabster near Thurso. From there it was a short car journey to the Queen Mother's residence at the Castle of Mey before rejoining the yacht at Scrabster and then on to Balmoral.

The young Prince would spend the mornings swimming with his mother at Ballater and then enjoy afternoon tea with his great grandmother. But it was the initial journey north aboard the celebrated vessel – to all intents and purposes a floating palace – that most excited William. He would often run riot around the elegant drawing room with its chintz-covered sofas, deep armchairs and luxurious Persian rugs, and finger the keys of the baby grand piano. Thankfully, his mother was a more accomplished pianist, her lullabies proving a calming influence on a young boy keen to let off steam.

William's ebullience was becoming something of a concern to the royal household. During his trip north, his parents were gravely concerned that 'Billy the Basher', as the press corps had affectionately nicknamed him, would wreak havoc in his great grandmother's presence. Certainly his boisterous, anti-social behaviour was getting worse: during one particular fire drill at Sandringham, he 'borrowed' a fireman's helmet and refused to hand it back. This public show of petulance brought home to Charles and Diana that their son was in need of more discipline and interaction with children of his own age.

In 1985 William, still only two years-old, makes his first flight without either parent on a trip from London to Aberdeen.

BALMORAL HAS BEEN THE SCOTTISH HOME OF THE ROYAL FAMILY SINCE IT WAS purchased for Queen Victoria by Prince Albert in 1852. He considered it too small so under his supervision a new building was designed. On 28 September 1853 the foundation stone was laid by Queen Victoria and the new castle – built from granite from the neighbouring quarries of Glen Gelder – was finally completed in 1856. When Queen Victoria died in 1901, the Balmoral estates passed, under the terms of her will, to King Edward VII and to each of his successors.

Although it remains largely the same as it was during Queen Victoria's reign, successive royal owners have made improvements to the estate. The Queen, the Duke of Edinburgh and Prince Charles take a passionate personal interest in the estate which, judging by his love for the area, will be continued by William.

The royal family disembark from *Britannia* at Aberdeen harbour after cruising the Western Isles, August 1985

AS 83RD IN A LONG LINE OF ROYAL YACHTS STRETCHING BACK TO 1660 AND THE reign of Charles II, **Britannia** holds a proud place in British maritime history. Launched at John Brown's Shipyard in Clydebank, Scotland on 16 April 1953 by Queen Elizabeth II, **Britannia** served monarch and country for 44 years, during which time she embarked on 968 official voyages, travelling a total of 1,087,623 nautical miles, and calling at over 600 ports in 135 countries. Each room, furnished to the Queen's personal taste, was filled with photographs of her children and grandchildren, treasured family heirlooms and personal possessions. This was the ship regarded by the royal family as their second home. Even with its full complement of (around 300) royal yachtsmen and royal household staff, the Queen commented that it was the one place where she felt she could truly relax.

  Britannia was to provide a honeymoon sanctuary for four couples in the world's most photographed family. Princess Margaret and Antony Armstrong-Jones were the first royal honeymooners to enjoy **Britannia**'s 5-star luxury in 1960 on their 6,000-mile voyage to the Caribbean. Following their wedding in 1973, Princess Anne and Captain Mark Phillips cruised the West Indies on **Britannia**, and in 1981, the Prince and Princess of Wales met the yacht in Gibraltar for their sixteen-day honeymoon voyage in the Mediterranean. Five years later **Britannia** hosted her final honeymoon – the Duke and Duchess of York spent five days cruising the Azores.

  At the beginning of January 1997, the yacht set sail from Portsmouth to Hong Kong on her last and longest voyage. On 11 December 1997 **Britannia** was decommissioned at Portsmouth Naval Base in the presence of the Queen, the Duke of Edinburgh and senior members of the royal family, ending 350 years of royal yachts. Four months later, after intense competition from cities around the UK, the government announced that, fittingly, **Britannia** would return to Scotland for her final berth. Owned by The Royal Yacht Britannia Trust, a charitable organisation, and permanently moored in Edinburgh's historic port of Leith, **Britannia** is now a major tourist attraction and corporate hospitality venue.

The Prince of Wales and William arrive at Aberdeen airport in August 1984. Unusually both the heir and the heir presumptive have flown together, something that will hardly ever happen again.

Early School Years

Calling on her own experiences of nursery day care, Diana was determined to find the school which best suited her child's needs. An extended period of research ended when non-uniformed police officers were spotted checking adjoining rooftops and fire escapes at 11 Chepstow Villas, Notting Hill Gate, West London, the Victorian terraced building which housed Mrs Jane Mynor's Nursery School.

Once again, Prince William broke with royal tradition by becoming the first future monarch to attend a private kindergarten. Mrs Mynor, the daughter of an Anglican bishop, admitted that she was 'surprised and delighted' by the Waleses decision – a decision influenced by the strongly felt opinions of the Princess who did not want her son's early education restricted to within the walls of Buckingham Palace.

William's first day at the £200-a term nursery school on 24 September 1985 became a huge media circus, with more than 60 reporters, television crews and photographers camped in the street. At precisely 9.40am, the young pupil arrived, fresh from his holiday at Balmoral and clutching a bright red Postman Pat children's flask full of orange. Met by Mrs Mynor, who promptly took her new charge by the hand, William entered through a door marked 'Cygnets' – later he would become a 'Little Swan' and, finally a 'Big Swan' but for now it was a handsome young prince who was spreading his wings. "This is William," she told Zoë, James, Fenelia and Max, who were busy making paper mice on the floor. This was the name by which the Prince would be known to his playmates during his time at the school.

The rest of the Cygnets made room for the new arrival with hardly a glance, while Diana looked through a glass door beaming with pride. It was her dream that her son should have as normal an education as possible and although obviously an 'upper class' establishment, three-year-old William was integrating with society and, more importantly, mixing with children of his own age. Charles and Diana looked anxious during the 10-minute drive back to Kensington Palace but they needn't have worried – 1 hour and 45 minutes later, the young Prince emerged, beaming with delight. Flagged by a detective, he had made a paper mouse for his parents. Mrs Mynor declared: "He did fine, he really liked it."

Charles wrote to all the Fleet Street editors, encouraging them to give William the privacy he needed to enjoy his education. Diana, meanwhile, made contact with the parents of the other 35 pupils; she did not want her son to be given preferential treatment. The windows of the nursery were replaced with

bulletproof glass and a panic button was installed next to Mrs Mynor's desk. William's detective accompanied him at every session and it was widely reported at the time that an armed guard was always in close proximity.

From his first day, William settled into his new surroundings with considerable ease. Although exuberant and even bossy towards his fellow pupils, he excelled in

cutting out pictures, model making, painting and singing. He played up to the crowd as a wolf in the school play – until he spotted his parents in the audience whereupon he burst out crying! When it came to more academic subjects, William was regarded as an average pupil. By all accounts he had a basic grasp of the 'Three Rs' by the time he left for Wetherby School, also in West London, however it wasn't until his teenage years that William showed more promise in his academic studies.

At school, William also began to excel in outdoor pursuits. His sporting interests would soon establish common ground with his father and he was taken to a polo match at the Guards Club, Windsor Castle in 1986. But children of that age have a short attention span and the young Prince was no different – pleading for ice cream and generally behaving badly in front of

We got the news that William was going to be taking part in his nursery school's nativity play and so bright and early on a very cold December morning I stood waiting. At first I thought I'd made a mistake because there was nobody else around – parents, police or other press. Lo and behold, suddenly William and his classmates emerged from the school to cross the road wearing their delightful little costumes. William was dressed as a shepherd. Strangely, I was still only one of two or three members of the press present. Actually I had got things mixed up and the official press call was for the following day, when, as it turned out, the children would not be wearing their costumes. It was one of those genuine, but really fortunate cock-ups. RN

the illustrious guests and photographers present. The first glimpses of Diana the disciplinarian were seen as she promptly smacked William and returned early to Kensington Palace. On another occasion while watching his father play polo at Windsor Great Park he pushed a little girl to the ground. Diana, patently embarrassed by the actions of her son, gave him a smack and within 20 minutes he was heading home yet again to Kensington Palace in a flood of tears!

William's tantrums were becoming all too commonplace – at nursery, he was often heard to say: "If you don't do what I say, then I'll have you arrested." At home, too, he had become unruly, a firebrand whose diatribes directed at the Kensington Palace staff would often leave his parents red-faced. In common with many four-year-olds, he would refuse to do what he was asked and would throw a wobbly when anyone attempted to discipline him.

During the wedding of his uncle, Prince Andrew, to Sarah Ferguson, Prince William again caused his parents acute embarrassment. While the other pageboys and bridesmaids demonstrated exemplary behaviour, William fidgeted throughout the ceremony and, in front of millions watching the occasion on TV worldwide, constantly poked his tongue out at whoever looked in his general direction.

For Charles in particular, it was the straw that broke the camel's back, and his initial reservations regarding Nanny Barnes's appointment and her liberal approach to the job now appeared to be justified. With William's imminent departure for Wetherby School, it was decided that Barnes should leave Kensington Palace, a decision with which Diana concurred willingly as she had become increasingly concerned – jealous even – of the bond that had developed between Barnes and William. The official statement from Buckingham Palace implied that the departure was a mutual decision.

For the next four weeks, Diana tried hard to ensure that her boys, naturally upset by the departure, would not miss 'Baba' too much. Public engagements were kept to a minimum as she involved herself in every aspect of their lives, from bathing and dressing to playing and cooking. By the time the announcement was made the following month that the new royal nanny would be Ruth Wallace, Diana had ensured a smooth transition.

Wallace's credentials were altogether more to Charles's liking. As a former nanny to the children of his close friend, King Constantine of Greece, 'Nanny Roof' made an instant impression with her more disciplined approach. She encouraged both William and Harry to be gracious to visitors to Kensington Palace and she was even given permission to smack the boys if necessary. By the time William moved to Wetherby in January 1987, his behaviour and decorum were considerably improved.

However, it would be wrong to single out Barnes as being totally to blame for William's rebellious nature. With his parents' unavoidable and extended absences, William simply failed to associate his parents with discipline – he saw only two people who showered him with love as compensation for their prolonged absences. William was also old enough now to detect the obvious tensions that had developed between his parents.

By the time William turned four, his parents' marriage had deteriorated to the point where they were effectively leading separate lives. The couple looked increasingly strained during public appearances together and an uneasy front was put on for the watching media. Yet behind the scenes, the battle lines had already been drawn. Charles had moved most of his belongings to his Gloucestershire residency, Highgrove, while Diana remained at Kensington Palace with her boys. The family would spend weekends together at the country retreat, where a truce was called for the sake of the children. An illusion of the happy family was played out and although the weekends were far removed from the fun-loving, outgoing lifestyle that was encouraged by his mother, William would grow to love the countryside.

Although the visits to Highgrove were comparatively brief, Charles made sure that both boys understood how life in the country worked and could be lived. Their time was filled with

"If you don't do what I say, then I'll have you arrested."

bike rides, country walks and pony trekking. Charles delighted in taking his son shooting and although too young to participate, William would, with his toy rifle, imitate his father; by the age of ten he would have been taught to use the real thing. At Highgrove he was able to roam free, away from the prying eyes of the public and press. He could scale fences and climb the highest trees and on one occasion had to be rescued by his detective!

William's life now seemed to embrace both the urban sophistication of his mother's world and the rural, even pastoral, retreat of his father. Nevertheless, his parents always met in the middle ground when it came to his education. In January 1987 he left Mrs Mynor's nursery for Wetherby, a £785-a-term pre-prep school just half a mile from Kensington Palace at Pembridge Square, Notting Hill. Accompanied by his mother (Charles was snowed in at Sandringham) and dressed in a uniform of grey overcoat and cap, grey and scarlet piped jacket, short trousers and three-quarter length socks, the Prince looked every inch like his mischievous TV namesake 'Just William' as he confidently climbed the steps for the first time, grinning and waving to photographers. He was greeted by headmistress Frederika Blair Turner before disappearing from sight to meet his teacher, Jane Ritchie, and his 19 fellow pupils.

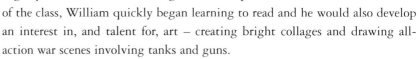

Had William been academically brighter, he would have been taken into Form One Green, but he was accompanied to Form One Red, a slightly less intense set. Although not the top of the class, William quickly began learning to read and he would also develop an interest in, and talent for, art – creating bright collages and drawing all-action war scenes involving tanks and guns.

William's air of confidence was never more evident than when he spoke in front of the rest of the class. One particular geography lesson involved the Queen's trip to China and he was particularly articulate as he gave something of an insider's account of Her Majesty's visit to the country's Great Wall. The six-year-old was also in good voice after taking the stage in the annual Christmas carol concert at the Palace Theatre in London's West End when he joined school friends in singing 16 carols, including a performance of Silent Night with two classmates. His parents joined other parents in singing four carols at the end of the concert – but there was no repeat of the tears or stage fright that had marked William's earlier stage appearance at Mrs Mynor's nursery!

His improved manners were also obvious as he opened the doors for his teachers, greeted guests by calling them 'sir' and 'madam' and doffing his cap whenever he saw Miss Blair Turner. But William's impish nature was never far

'Just William!'

from the surface and he quickly earned a reputation as a practical joker. 'Basher', as he was now widely called, once typed the words 'WEE' and 'BOTTOM' (spelled BOTEM) into the classroom computer, earning him a scolding from his teacher and widespread approval from his growing band of friends. On another occasion he was reprimanded for not wearing his school tie.

By all accounts, William's favourite school dinner was mince, potatoes and ravioli, and he was always in the thick of the action when it came to the rough and tumble of the playground – he liked nothing better than kicking a football around in the adjacent, yet secluded, Pembridge Square Garden. Certainly sport was playing an ever-increasing role in the young Prince's life and in the annual Wetherby sports day at the Richmond Athletics track in Surrey he invariably won every running race he entered – the Prince and Princess of Wales also took part in the parents' races. When not participating in a sporting activity, William's energy would be channelled into playing other games – in his third year at the school, he felt the back of his mother's hand yet again when he ran away to play a game of tag when he should have gone home. After calling him for a third time – and being totally ignored – Diana followed him onto the field and gave him a sharp smack. William promptly burst into tears.

William's exuberance was a reflection of his love for life and the great outdoors. Together with his mother, he would continue to enjoy many afternoons swimming at Buckingham Palace or at Diana's Chelsea health club. He shared her passion for tennis and would sometimes accompany her to the royal box at Wimbledon. More bizarrely, he also developed an interest in supporting Aston Villa Football Club. Football is not a sport normally associated with the royal family, yet William played for Wetherby and was renowned for his tough tackling and precision passing. In one particular game, against Bassett House of Kensington, his man-of-the-match performance was the highlight of a 2–1 win on a bumpy park pitch at Wormwood Scrubs, West London, leaving Bassett sports master Steve Baric to gush "If he carries on in that manner, he could develop into a very good prospect. He did very well and was not afraid to get stuck in."

Like many boys of his age, he had a passion for go-karting and skateboarding. To the delight of his father, he also continued the royal tradition of equestrian excellence, learning to ride his Shetland ponies –

Not for the first time the considerable ebullience of 'Billy the Basher' has earned him a smack on the bottom.

Smokey and Trigger – bareback by the age of four. Within a year he could ride while standing in the saddle. By the age of seven he greatly impressed Charles by learning to 'beat the brush' – the art of drawing pheasants towards the shoot.

However, his exuberance triggered an amazing security scare when, on one particular visit to Balmoral, he headed for the hills on his pony and it was the best part of an hour before a royal detective noticed that he was no longer playing with his brother. Princess Anne's children, Zara and Peter, set off to find him. Fortunately he was found watching some soldiers working near the castle; he was hauled back home where he received another ticking off from his mother.

William also gained immense pleasure from riding his trusted BMX bike and looked the picture of happiness as he joined his parents and brother on a bike ride during a half-term holiday break in the Scilly Isles in 1989; another example of his parents attempting to create some semblance of normal family life. Despite the purposely instilled sense of 'normality', there was no escaping the fact that William's life would never be conventional. Like his mother, his every public move would be scrutinised.

One of the earliest indications of the unprecedented levels of media interest that would, if left unregulated, overwhelm the young royal came during a break in Spain in August 1987. With bucket and spade at the ready, William and Harry were ready for a day out with the family of ex-King Constantine of Greece. But as they neared the sea at Alcudia, on the north Majorcan coast, their security guards were forced to cancel the trip. Clearly disappointed, William stormed off and the party was forced to spend the rest of the day at King Juan Carlos's summer residence, Marivent Palace, just outside Palma, the only respite they could get from the massed media. It transpired that Spanish journalists had tailed the young princes in seven cars, ignoring pleas by Buckingham Palace and the King of Spain that the family should be left in peace. It was the start of a very cool relationship between the Prince and the media and a portent of the difficulties he would face trying to lead a life free from prying eyes.

Although Diana was distraught when William packed his bags for boarding school at Ludgrove in 1990, the timing of his departure was opportune. Not only had the media interest in the royal couple continued unabated, the relationship between his parents had by now reached breaking point and the speculation surrounding the true nature of the marriage was at fever pitch. Diana took the disintegration of her marriage particularly hard and would often break down in the presence of her two sons. Although Harry was too young to

Above: Under the expert eye of Princess Anne and her children Zara and Peter, William learns to ride at Sandringham in 1987. William has become a skilled and enthusiastic rider like so many members of the royal family.

Opposite page: A nearly five-year-old William hurls stones into the River Dee near the Queen Mother's lodge at Ballater, while Charles looks on and Harry plays among the rocks.

comprehend the seriousness of the situation, William became an understanding friend as well as a son. Hearing his mother sobbing one weekend at Highgrove, he considerately popped a few tissues under the door, while on another occasion he showed his growing maturity by booking a table for two at Diana's favourite restaurant, San Lorenzo, in an attempt to cheer her up.

Having completed three years at Wetherby, Ludgrove would become William's sanctuary as much as the next step on the educational ladder. The decision to send him to the preparatory school near Wokingham again swept aside years of royal tradition; despite the Queen's wish that William should attend Gordonstoun, he would not be following his father and grandfather to that bleak Scottish outpost.

His parents had made two visits to the Eton 'feeder' school in leafy Berkshire and were immediately impressed by the well-run establishment, which was founded in 1892 and lists the Dukes of Kent and Wellington among its old boys. Diana, in particular, delighted in the fact that the school frowns on corporal punishment and spurns traditional uniforms. With the added advantage of its reasonably close proximity to both Kensington Palace and Highgrove, it seemed an obvious choice and security measures were quickly put in place, including the erection of high fences around the main building, the re-fencing of the 130-acre grounds and the installation of closed circuit television.

On William's first day, 10 September 1990, accompanied by both his parents, he looked dignified, confident and immaculately turned out in his maroon cords and grey V-neck sweater, the epitome of a young royal. As he shook hands with joint headmaster, Gerald Barber, there was little to indicate how incredibly tough he would find his initial term. William may have found the separation from his parents difficult, but Diana was to feel his absence keenly and was visibly close to tears as she left the Ludgrove gates that autumnal afternoon.

That William would struggle to adapt to his new surroundings was inevitable given the leisurely life to which he had become accustomed with his parents and brother. Phone calls to parents were barred, except in an emergency, and he would only return home every four weeks and during school holidays. A typical day for the Prince started at 7.15am and ended with bedtime at 8.00pm, with only 40 minutes of free time during the day in which he would be permitted to watch closely monitored TV programmes. William was often seen in tears during his first few weeks so, in an effort to ease the pain for both mother and son, Diana was allowed frequent visits in his first term. She would learn that as a new boy, her son 'Wills' was now known as a 'squit', in Year Two he would be known as a 'squirt', as he got older he would become a 'jolly good fellow' before ending his education as a 'jolly jolly, good fellow'!

She took a keen interest in William's timetable that included English, Latin, maths and computer studies. The sports-mad Prince played football, rugby, basketball, Eton fives, fencing and riding. He was also a stylish swimmer, a good clay pigeon shot and represented the school at cross-country running. The growing of flowers and vegetables was encouraged – much to the delight of William's gardening-mad father! The pupils were usually addressed by their surname but the Prince was addressed as William. As time progressed William began to evolve from a somewhat tearful boy to a delightfully mannered young man, but he was still regarded as a somewhat aloof figure, behaviour almost certainly linked to the very public problems engulfing his parents' marriage. Although shielded from the outside media by Mr Barber, adolescent boys can be cruel and the gossip-mongering soon took hold. William

would often use the 30-minute exercise time after breakfast to stroll in the grounds and compose his thoughts. It was a testament to his strong character that he never allowed his personal worries to affect his education.

Indeed, he blossomed into a model academic student, finishing regularly in the top third of his class and being appointed as a class monitor. His sporting talent began to shine as he became the school's star basketball player while continuing his passion for swimming and football. He had also discovered a new sport, golf. However, one particular afternoon in June 1991, an incident on the school's very own nine-hole golf course created headline news as the first real drama in the young royal's life.

As one of his friends swung a club, it struck William just above his left eye and he collapsed to the ground with blood pouring from the wound. Against the school's wishes his personal protection officer, Reg Spinney, decided to call an ambulance and William was rushed to the Royal Berkshire Hospital. Doctors diagnosed a depressed fracture of the forehead which would require specialist neurosurgery. The warring Waleses put aside their personal grievances to rush to the aid of their elder son and after consultation with the hospital's senior doctor, it was decided that William would be transferred to

During the tour to Canada in October 1991, it became increasingly obvious that Diana was no longer the centre of attraction; the whole world seemed to be looking at the boys. In fact it's almost impossible to find a picture of Prince Charles who was, of course, there the whole time. Interestingly, when Charles and the boys returned to Canada nearly seven years later, it was William who stole the show – the start of 'Willsmania'. On this occasion Diana chose to take William and Harry to Niagara Falls, where they had a marvellous time on the *Maid of the Mist* and we, and they, got thoroughly soaked. RN

London's Great Ormond Street Hospital. The successful 70-minute operation was carried out under general anaesthetic.

A tearful Diana cancelled a visit to Yorkshire to remain at her son's bedside that night, but Charles decided to adhere to his schedule and attend a performance of the opera *Tosca* at Covent Garden. This decision was greeted with widespread condemnation in the tabloids and he was branded as an uncaring father, despite the fact that he was kept informed of his son's health via a pager. Diana was portrayed as the more loving parent of the two, caring for her son at Kensington Palace where he convalesced for two weeks before returning to Ludgrove, never to pick up a golf club again.

Diana's obvious love for both her sons could not be called into question, but more cynical observers would suggest that she played up to the cameras to score points against her husband. On one particular trip to Canada, protocol again dictated that the boys had to travel separately from their parents – together with new nanny Jessie Webb – and although Diana had only been parted from her sons for 24 hours, she literally ran across the deck of *Britannia* in Toronto to greet the boys. Naturally, William fell into the arms of his mother first, then it was Harry's turn for a kiss and a squeeze. As far as Diana was concerned, no one could match her love for her sons. If her marriage was to end in divorce, she was determined to maintain a vice-like grip on the boys. It was her responsibility to ensure the boys' welfare and to raise them to become respected members and leaders of society – they would not be handed over to the royal family without a fight.

The highlight of William's first official family trip abroad came when he escorted his mother to a gala presentation of the musical *Les Misérables* in Toronto and stood in a reception line with her to meet the 45 VIPs attending. Although visits to Niagara Falls and aboard the Canadian battleship *Ottawa* were also included in the itinerary, later during the trip William would be introduced to some 60 politically and socially prominent guests aboard *Britannia*. The grooming of the future king had begun in earnest.

As proof of Diana's immense pride in her eldest son, she decided that at the age of eight he was ready for his first official engagement. As the future Prince of Wales, it was considered appropriate that his inaugural trip should be to Cardiff on St David's Day, 1 March 1991. Wearing the traditional Welsh emblem, the daffodil, he greeted the huge crowds who lined the streets in his honour. Yet again, his father was conspicuous by his absence. Charles was visiting the wives of military personnel at a base nearby, so it was left to Diana, by now an experienced hand at greeting the public, to guide her son through the crowds of well-wishers. William appeared to cope admirably until one young girl, Lucy Willis, handed him a bouquet of daffodils whereupon he turned to his mother blushing furiously. He would also unveil a plaque promoting Welsh culture before signing a guestbook,

Like many of his ancestors, William is obviously left-handed as he signs a guestbook in Cardiff.

where it became apparent William was left-handed, following a long line of royals including George II, George VI, Queen Victoria, Queen Elizabeth the Queen Mother and his father.

Having also attended the Wales v France rugby match at the Cardiff Arms Park, his bond with the country had been cemented.

In November the Queen proclaimed 1992 her *annus horribilis* following the break-up not only of Charles's marriage but also that of the Duke and Duchess of York (Prince Andrew and Sarah Ferguson), and the disastrous fire at her beloved Windsor Castle. William would also suffer the loss of his grandfather, Earl Spencer, another trauma that would only serve to draw the 10-year-old closer to his mother.

On 9 December 1992, the nation's worst fears were realised when Prime Minister John Major announced to the House of Commons the separation of the Prince and Princess of Wales. "This decision has been reached amicably," he said, "and they will both continue to participate fully in the upbringing of their children. The Queen and the Duke of Edinburgh, though saddened, understand and sympathise with the difficulties that have led to this decision. Her Majesty and His Royal Highness particularly hope the intrusions into the privacy of the Prince and Princess may now cease. They believe that a degree of privacy and understanding is essential if Their Royal Highnesses are to provide a happy and secure upbringing for their children ..."

Although too young to be fully cognisant of all the facts, William believed Diana to be the innocent victim in the break-up of the marriage. His growing antipathy towards the press was further fuelled by the intense scrutiny under which both his mother and father now found themselves. Following news of the separation, it was rare to pick up a paper, particularly the tabloid press, without a sensationalised story involving either parent and William would later confess that whenever he saw a picture of his parents in print, his heart would sink and a sick feeling would develop in the pit of his stomach.

Later that Winter, on a trip to the Austrian ski resort of Lech, matters came

We had been told that Diana would be going officially to the old Cardiff Arms Park for the Wales v France rugby match in February 1992. On something of a wing and prayer I travelled to Wales hoping she would take the boys and was, as things turned out, just about the only representative of the London press who made the trip. At the end of the game I went down underneath the stands and was amazed at how hospitable the South Wales constabulary were – obviously they were keen to be photographed with the boys. So just before Diana and the boys left they put on a show wearing police hats and uniforms and sitting on police motorbikes. It made for a great photo opportunity. The film was back in London and processed that Saturday night, the pictures syndicated worldwide on Sunday. RN

The widening chasm between Charles and Diana was put to one side as the couple took their sons to Lech in March 1992. But their joy on the slopes came to an abrupt halt when Diana was told that her father, the 68-year-old eighth Earl Spencer, had died of a heart attack in London. Although the Earl had been admitted to the Humana Wellington Hospital with pneumonia, it was believed he was on the path to recovery and the news of his death hit Diana particularly hard. She had a very close relationship with her father, who had raised his four children after divorcing in 1969. Looking devastated, Diana left Lech the next morning with Charles. Three days later, over 100 relatives and friends were present for the funeral near the family home at Althorp and although William and Harry were spared that occasion, they were present at a memorial service held at St Margaret's Church in May.

to a head when William and Harry were embroiled in what was dubbed 'The Battle of Lech'. As they emerged with their mother from a sweet shop, all three were blitzed by a swarm of mainly European photographers. Diana, fearing that her boys might be trampled, put her arms around them while her bodyguard, Inspector Ken Wharfe, fended off the crowd. One persistent Italian snapper was pushed to the ground.

William, in particular, was clearly upset as the party returned to the confines of the Arlberg Hotel; at school they had been sheltered from such treatment. The following morning, Harry and Diana had apparently managed to shrug off the incident but William kept his head down, withdrew into his blue padded coat and refused to smile for an official photoshoot. He was rumoured to mutter "I wish I wasn't here" before disappearing into the distance. Away from the cameras, however, William was able to just be himself as he built igloos and indulged in snowball fights with his brother, friend Harry Soames, Inspector Wharfe and ski instructor Markus Kleissl. Diana joined in these games enthusiastically, but as a result of a vicious pincer movement by her sons, she usually ended up with a snowball to the back of the head!

The incident at Lech was an example of the press at its worst, and when the hysteria was virtually repeated the following year, William – now a year older and a year wiser – decided to take matters into his own hands. His mother had been visibly shaken by the constant hounding and when a group of photographers ignored an agreement that no more pictures would be taken of the Princess on that particular day, he skied over and took them to task. The fiery side of his nature became apparent for the first time as he threatened to confiscate their cameras and equipment, stating "Just leave my mother alone". Only the intervention of a royal security guard prevented the situation from escalating. This was the clearest sign yet of William's antagonism towards the tabloid press.

Certainly, he had developed a deep mistrust of the press in general and had discovered that if he gave an inch, they would take a mile. As a young boy, he had been more than happy to pose for arranged photocalls with his family, but as he grew up he became aware that even when the cameras had stopped clicking, an unscrupulous few remained who failed to play by the rules. William felt his rights to live freely and enjoy himself were being infringed.

On holiday at the Costa del Sol, William and his brother were all set to spend a day messing about on boats and jet skis. Their walk down to the water's edge would take them past the assembled ranks of photographers. Harry's enthusiasm for the day on the water never waivered for a moment, taking little notice of the press contingent, but William again bowed his head, shielding his face with his hand – he would no longer play ball with the press. The stubborn side of his nature was evident for all to see. Yet when he had something to show the press, William showed he had learnt some of his mother's skill at presenting the image he wanted to get across. The next day William swam out to a motor launch hired by several enterprising British photographers, giving a superb display of his skilful swimming technique; providing a unique series of photographs, a happy photographer and a satisfied Fleet Street – for a while at least.

Regular trips with Diana were commonplace as a means of helping to heal the boys' wounds from the break-up of the marriage. For William, they also provided a welcome release from Ludgrove. America was a favoured destination of the Princess and as details of the breakdown of the marriage became common knowledge, William had travelled to the US for what was dubbed his 'Wild West' holiday. While there he liked nothing better than feasting on his favourite 'Loony Burger' – a massive 6-inch burger in a bun, topped with fries, piles of fried mushrooms and three types of cheese.

Diana had also taken her sons to Orlando, Florida in August 1993, accompanied by the usual travelling media circus. The boys had already acquired a taste for the thrills and spills of amusement parks following a trip to Thorpe Park in Surrey, but that experience would be eclipsed by a trip to Disney World. Diana had promised her sons a 'holiday of a lifetime' and she did not disappoint. The boys met Mickey Mouse, Donald Duck and Pluto, they visited the three themed parks: the Magical Kingdom, the futuristic Epcot Centre and the Disney MGM studios. The highlight of the trip, however, had to be the Typhoon Lagoon water fun park, claimed to be the biggest of its kind in the world.

This trip was in many ways a resounding success, especially for the boys who enjoyed it enormously and was another example of Diana's determination to give her boys a chance to experience a 'normal life'.

William in particular was always closely associated with his mother, not least because of his striking physical resemblance to her that was becoming more apparent in his early teens. Yet he also enjoyed the time he spent with other members of the royal family and, as the future heir to throne, he began to realise that the pomp and ceremony that he so disliked played a huge role in their everyday life and had to be learnt and respected. Trips to Florida and the like were all well and good, but would they really prepare him for his future role as king?

The first Christmas following the separation of his parents was spent at Sandringham with Charles and Harry, while Diana joined her brother at Althorp. In his early years, William had found the presence of his grandmother somewhat daunting, but as he matured he began to warm to her and the Duke of Edinburgh, to understand the role of the royal family in society – and, indeed, his own position as future heir to the throne. He made a point of having tea with the Queen each week at Buckingham Palace, while the Duke showed him the finer points of shooting.

At church that Christmas, William escorted the Queen Mother into the chapel of St Mary Magdalene. In accordance with royal etiquette, he would now bow in his grandmother's presence and address all royal servants and members of staff

A 10-year-old William relishes the end of an exhilarating ride at Thorpe Park.

in the correct manner. When dining he had to dress formally, hold his knife and fork correctly and was not allowed to talk or begin eating until instructed to do so by his elders. To his mother, this was a pompous and archaic way to conduct everyday life in the 20th century, but William was beginning to understand the traditions of the royal family and to behave in accordance with them.

The separation did, in fact, bring William closer to his father, who made a concerted effort to spend as many weekends as possible with both his sons. At home with his mother, he watched his favourite TV programme *Mr Bean* and played with his model dinosaurs, spaceships and his Nintendo games console. As

The Queen Mother, Diana and William at the Trooping the Colour in 1989. The Queen Mother was always a ready source of encouragement and advice to the young Prince as he grew up.

a contrast, in his father's company he would find time to read books and ask questions about wildlife, geography and the great outdoors – subjects on which Charles is very knowledgeable.

With William close to his eleventh birthday, Charles took his eldest son on his first hunting expedition. Having learned the logistics of shooting from his days at Balmoral, he was handed a single-barrel shotgun and proceeded to shoot six rabbits in just two hours. Needless to say, this controversial pursuit hit the front pages of the following day's newspapers. Animal Rights activists were outraged at the actions of the young Prince. "It's a crying shame that yet another generation of the royal family is being raised to be degenerate," moaned John Robbins, head of Animal Concern, "I'm sure his mother doesn't approve."

Certainly, Diana was ahead on points when it came to the public's perception of a loving parent. There could be no doubting Charles's important role in raising the future heir, but when it came to a hug, a joke or an afternoon of adolescent fun, then it was Diana to whom William would turn. He would run into his mother's room in the morning and jump on her – a pillow fight invariably followed. He delighted in playing games of tag with his mother and brother, and the huge Kensington Palace apartments provided a marvellous environment for hide and seek – a particular favourite.

Charles, obviously aware of the lack of a maternal presence at Highgrove, decided it was time to find a 'surrogate mother' to whom the boys could relate. Easter 1993 saw the appointment of Tiggy Legge-Bourke, an associate of Prince Charles who was to become William's best friend. Although officially appointed as an assistant to Charles's private secretary, Commander Richard Aylard, in reality she would become a friend, confidante and aide. Like Diana, she was very outgoing, forward-thinking and, at the age of 30, still young enough to be able to identify with a young person's needs and outlook. She also loved to fish, ski, shoot and ride, all of which pleased Charles immensely.

Charles was first introduced to Tiggy when she was just six – her mother, Shan, was employed as a lady-in-waiting to Princess Anne. The daughter of an extremely rich merchant banker, she grew up on the family estate, Glanusk Park in Wales, and as a young girl, attended a convent school run by Ursuline nuns. She then moved to the Manor House in Dunford, a prep school run by Lady Tryon (mother-in-law of Charles's friend, Lady 'Kanga' Tryon). By the time she had turned 13, Tiggy – real name Alexandra – enrolled at Heathfield, an elite boarding school in Ascot before completing her education at the Institut Alpin Videmanette, near Gstaad in Switzerland, which coincidentally was the same school that Diana had attended.

Although gifted athletically, Tiggy was not particularly academic having gained only four GCE O levels. Her career would, in fact, run parallel with that of the Princess. She attended a Montessori kindergarten course before opening her own nursery in Battersea, South London in 1985 named Mrs Tiggywinkles after the famous hedgehog character in the Beatrix Potter books, hence the nickname 'Tiggy'. Later the school had to close, but Tiggy had proved she had the qualities needed to care and bond with young children. A very natural, unpretentious young woman, Charles believed she had the right qualities to be trusted with the future welfare of his children.

Within months, she had developed a strong bond with the boys, particularly with William, who saw her more as an older sister than a replacement for his beloved mother. The bitterness between his parents obviously affected him deeply, but whenever he visited Highgrove or Balmoral, Tiggy would be there to lift his spirits by climbing trees, indulging in mock fights and, more often than not, beating him at football.

There could be no doubting Charles's important role in raising the future heir, but when it came to a hug, a joke or an afternoon of adolescent fun, then it was Diana to whom William would turn.

In the Easter following William and Harry's trip to Disney World, Charles pulled out all the stops to ensure that his sons' break at the Queen Mother's home at Birkhall would be unlike any other trip they had previously encountered at the usually staid 18th-century Scottish residency. A week before the boys were due to arrive, a container lorry arrived carrying a set of football goalposts, a badminton set, two mountain bikes, a huge trampoline, guns for shooting rabbits and two quad bikes, worth in the region of £2,000 each. Not surprisingly, it was Tiggy who was responsible for advising Charles on the boys' needs and she was the one who kept them amused throughout their stay.

Diana was becomingly increasingly concerned at Tiggy's growing influence on her young sons. Whether it was Highgrove, Balmoral, Sandringham or skiing in Klosters, Tiggy would be present and her closeness to William, in particular, caused the Princess great consternation. The relationship between the pair had grown so strong that the young Prince was now confiding in his 'older sis' on a whole host of topics that he felt his parents would find difficult to comprehend. He was aware of his mother's distaste for many of the royal pursuits in which he was now indulging on a regular basis with his father, especially Diana's disapproval of blood sports. As a crack shot, Tiggy accompanied William on many of his shooting trips, further fuelling the bitterness Diana now felt towards her.

Diana's insecurities were to prove unfounded. There was absolutely no one who could replace her in William's affections, and his respect for her deepened as he began to understand and take a keen interest in the many charitable organisations for whom she worked. He marvelled as she held babies who were undergoing chemotherapy, hugged AIDS patients and wept openly as she was told first-hand stories of women who had suffered abuse at the hands of their husbands. Diana was above all a very caring woman who encouraged William to share her compassion towards other people. At a very tender age he had become a shoulder she could lean on, her confidant — in the absence of a husband, perhaps even her soul mate.

William was just 11 years of age when he accompanied his mother on a private visit to The Passage, a refuge for the homeless near Westminster Cathedral. Diana could show the world that her son — the future king — would, indeed, share her passion for helping the underprivileged and the needy. He did not disappoint, showing maturity beyond his years as he mingled with the down-and-outs — he even managed his own walkabout under the guidance of Sister Bridie Down, principal of The Passage who said of the Prince: "He carried it off with what I can only describe as great style."

This appearance, in particular, elicited both praise and surprise from royal watchers: never before had a royal undertaken this type of engagement at such a young age. Life had been very different for his father; at the same age he, like William, was at prep school but when the young Prince Charles made a public appearance with his parents, he had to be ready waiting for them exactly one minute before they arrived — and not a second later. The Queen and Duke of Edinburgh's reasoning was that if Charles established good timekeeping habits

Diana's insecurities were to prove unfounded. There was absolutely no one who could replace her in William's affections.

at a young age, he would find it easier to cope with the rigid timetable to which he would have to adhere in the future when his diary would be packed with endless royal engagements. In comparison, William's life was relatively informal. Boarding school and visits to his grandmother's stately houses were punctuated by his trips to Disney World, Thorpe Park and the laughter and jokes that had become an integral part of his upbringing at Kensington Palace.

For Charles at that age, the highlight of his year would be a backstage pass at the Victoria Palace theatre to pull a few puppet strings. His dress would be formal – even for such an informal visit, he would always wear a tie. William, on the other hand, was aware of the latest fashion trends and was often seen wearing designer trainers, sweatshirts and baseball caps; suits were only brought out for more formal occasions. William was being moulded into a modern, model prince for the 21st century.

With the dust settling after the breakdown of his parents' marriage, and his life now following a pattern of relative normality, William's performances at Ludgrove improved significantly. In the immediate weeks and months that followed the separation, his achievements, both in and outside the classroom had tailed off dramatically. But supported by the love and affection being provided by both his parents, and by virtue of his hard work, the young Prince passed his Common Entrance Exam for Eton. He was also helped, in no small part, by a ruling that barred the press from intruding on his studies.

Free from any press intrusion, William could be himself and he would soon become 'one of the lads'. He had no wish to be treated differently from his fellow pupils and made a point of insisting that everyone called him 'Wills', going to great lengths to ensure that none of his peers were upset by, jealous or even tired of, his presence.

William was certainly frustrated by having a team of police protection officers accompany his every move. They slept in an adjoining room at Ludgrove and were his constant companions. Although by and large he and the officers got on well, like any teenager, William needed his own space – but wherever he went, his protection squad would be there. The first signs of real antipathy towards the omnipresent security, which manifested itself as outright antagonism, was seen during the skiing trip at Lech. After a day's sledging and just after sunset, William took off from the top of a steep hill, completely unaware that the road at the foot of the slope was a throughway for local vehicles. Suddenly, from nowhere, one of the detectives threw himself onto the speeding sledge, averting possible disaster. Far from showing gratitude, William was livid. "Why do I have to be surrounded by policemen all the time? Why won't you let me be a normal person?" he moaned.

William would sometimes 'slip his lead' and disappear into the grounds of the school, leaving his protectors panic-stricken and fearful that the future king had been abducted. As this prank became more and more frequent, William's guards were left with no alternative other than to report this behaviour to Charles directly, who was called to the school immediately to talk to his son.

The Princess of Wales and William go shopping in Cirencester near Highgrove in the spring of 1992.

On another occasion, William was said to have held a fellow student's head down the toilet and flushed it: the ideal punishment, he felt, for someone telling tales about his parents. Again, he was hauled over the coals and told by his headmaster not to repeat this understandable but not entirely appropriate behaviour! But these acts of indiscipline were few and far between as William coasted through his final year. He scored over 65 per cent to ensure a safe passage into Eton, although he failed in his attempts to score a distinction. For a young boy about to enter his teens, the curriculum was obviously more difficult than the average state comprehensive, yet William managed to balance his tough academic schedule with a life outside the classroom. For his final year, he had become a prefect, which entitled him to the rare pleasure of having a radio in his room. His renewed confidence showed when he gave a reading before an audience of several hundred students and parents at the 1994 Christmas carol service.

William continued to excel on the sports field; he was widely regarded as a consistently high-scoring middle-order batsman for the school's cricket XI, while his tough tackling made him a certainty in the centre of midfield or defence for the football team. He also captained the rugby and hockey teams, but in his final term, it would be tennis to which he took a particular shine. He shared this passion for tennis with Diana, and was seen on more than one occasion in the royal box during Wimbledon fortnight. William first caught the bug watching Steffi Graf on her way to winning the 1991 title, and he would often play against his mother in his spare time at the exclusive Harbour Health Club in Chelsea.

As his days at Ludgrove came to a close, the pair took part in a mother and son tennis competition, which gave the world's media a rare glimpse into life behind closed doors at the school and the passion they both shared for the sport. Although they failed to win the competition, William showed a mean sliced backhand – left-handed of course – and was forever urging his mother, jokingly, to raise her game. William also partnered his father in a clay pigeon shoot at Ludgrove that summer, an event which largely went unnoticed.

Exams also meant William could enjoy the rare privilege of weekends at home which, in his case, meant one day in London, the other at his father's estate. Although contrasting experiences, they were equally rewarding: life was fairly laid back at Highgrove with long brisk walks or endless hours of riding if Tiggy was around. Educational videos and readings of Kipling were encouraged. At Kensington Palace with Diana, the pace changed; swimming, tennis and dinners at the Chicago Rib Shack in Kensington, dressed in his favoured jeans, baseball jacket and cap were the order of the day.

On one occasion when he accompanied his mother and a friend to a Wales v Ireland rugby match, he was caught red-handed poring over a magazine spread detailing the lives of Playboy pin-ups Shane and Sia (the Barbi twins). Although initially rather shocked, Diana was unable to keep a straight face and the reprimand degenerated into fits of laughter – another example of her more liberal approach to bringing up her sons. At this stage in his life, William had far more in common with his mother than Prince Charles.

It was always Diana's desire to give her children as normal an upbringing as was humanly possible. Whether it was a trip to Alton Towers, a visit to the West End to see the latest film or even a trip on London's Underground system, she did so with her sons' future roles in mind. Diana was respectful of William's royal destiny, extremely proud that one day he would be king. Having seen at first hand the results of Charles's resricted childhood, she was determined to give her boys the chance to experience everyday life. A trip to the boy's favourite eatery, the Chicago Rib Shack, was a typical example of Diana's influence.

Eton Years

The year 1995 would prove a watershed in the young life of Prince William. A teenager in July, he made another quantum leap just three months later when his life began at Eton, the most famous and celebrated public school of them all.

Situated by the River Thames near Windsor in Berkshire, Eton College was founded in 1440 by Henry VI and has been responsible for the education of the sons of Europe's most well-heeled and powerful families. Immersed in tradition, Eton has produced one Northern Ireland and eighteen British prime ministers. It teaches most languages of the world, including ancient Greek and Latin, and computer studies, cookery – even car maintenance – are also on the curriculum. It is a wonderful establishment for sport, catering for all the traditional British sports as well as rowing, fives, racquets and the unique and bizarre Eton Wall game, in which a wall is defended in large numbers by the 'Collegers' against their attacking younger 'Oppidan' rivals – even though there has been no score for decades!

Yet what truly sets Eton apart from its contemporaries is the uniform; all the boys go about their daily life wearing pinstripe trousers, a waistcoat, stiff white collars and tails. Casual clothes are only worn when the boys go into Windsor during their free time, and they are forbidden to remain off-site after the twilight hours. Students spend their evenings in the twenty-four houses which accommodate in the region of fifty pupils each. Although the regime may appear strict by modern-day standards, over the years the rules and restrictions have been, to some extent, relaxed. It is a forward-thinking establishment, which prides itself on the academic achievements of its pupils, many of whom now come from varying social and ethnic backgrounds. Indeed, it was this positive and ecumenical attitude which most impressed Charles when he visited the school before William's arrival. Looking back at his own school days at Gordonstoun, Charles recalled that for him it was not unusual to have to endure an ice cold shower on a winter's morning before being forced to play rugby on snow-laden pitches in the skimpiest of clothes. He regarded his time at Gordonstoun as 'a prison sentence' and had no wish to see his children suffer the same misery and discomfort. He was also proud that his son would be following in the footsteps of the Duke of Kent and his son the Earl of St Andrews, who had passed through Eton with flying colours. Diana, too, was more than happy: her brother and father were Old Etonians and the College is just a 30-minute journey from Kensington Palace, much closer than Ludgrove.

To all intents and purposes, Eton would become a second family for William during one of the most testing periods of his life. Housemaster, Dr Andrew Gailey, would guide him; his private tutor, Mr Stuart-Clarke, would advise him while Elizabeth Heathcote, who was the house matron, eventually rivalled Tiggy Legge-Bourke as the most important female – other than his mother – in the young Prince's life.

Dr Gailey made education and discipline his key responsibilities while Stuart-Clarke would spend two hours in William's company each week discussing his progress, minor problems and relationships with other boys in the House. But it was Elizabeth Heathcote, herself a daughter of an old Etonian, who became a maternal figure. She would hand out treats such as Mars bars, but wouldn't hesitate to bring the boys into line if they strayed too far from the straight and narrow. William respected her deeply and regarded her as his rock. In the early days he leaned heavily on her: she would always be on hand to provide such essentials as toothpaste, socks and stationery or help with attaching the stiff shirt collars. She would sit with all the younger boys at lunch and would supervise the friendships William would make. She would play an important role in helping to shape the future king.

No ordinary first day at a new school – a nerve-racking time for anyone – but with hundreds of press, photographers and well-wishers watching his every move, William has every right to look nervous on his arrival at Eton. Although he looked more than happy the next day in the unique Eton uniform of pinstripe trousers, waistcoat, stiff white collars and tails.

At 4.15pm on Wednesday 6 September 1995, William arrived at Eton, unaccompanied by his luggage or belongings, which had been delivered in advance. He looked rather tense as he paused briefly with his parents and Elizabeth Heathcote for the cameras and it took a couple of whispers from his mother and brother for him to relax and smile ruefully. Dr Gailey led the party into the main building where William was introduced to Eton's headmaster, New Zealander John Lewis, before signing the entrance book. He was meant to sign 'HRH Prince William' in alphabetical order after another new boy, Wickrama Singhe. In his excitement, however, he signed after Keith Chung Pi

Wu, leaving his father grinning nervously, his mother in fits of laughter and Eton's latest arrival red-cheeked and somewhat embarrassed.

The parting from his parents took place behind closed doors before William was escorted to his new living quarters in the four-storey Manor House. For the next five years his rather modest accommodation would be a small 10 x 7 ft bedroom with adjoining study, which he livened up with a host of posters, mainly of his favourite pin-ups: Pamela Anderson, Cindy Crawford and, of course, the Barbi twins! As the future king, he did enjoy one privilege over other pupils, his own bathroom, but apart from this one luxury he was treated in exactly the same way as the other forty-nine boys in his house – very much according to William's own wishes.

However, there would always be one visible difference – the Prince's accompanying protection officers who had become part and parcel of his academic life. But if he thought the protection he had experienced at Ludgrove was overbearing, it was nothing compared to Eton, where he would receive 'round the clock' protection. Eton is easily accessible by public roads making it extremely difficult to police. As at Ludgrove, a royal protection officer would sleep in an adjacent room and wherever William went in the school grounds, he would be accompanied by at least two more armed officers, albeit at a reasonable distance.

With the town of Windsor just a stone's throw from Eton, William would often walk into the town with his friends for a visit to a local café or teashop and, obviously, the protection officers would follow closely behind. With the streets packed with tourists as well as local residents, security would be stepped up even further and it wasn't unusual for the boys to have a police officer literally breathing down their necks. Although not an ideal adjunct to the life of a teenager, as he got older William began to appreciate the necessity of protection; but his friends must have found it an unusual and frustrating experience in those early days.

But William was not alone when it came to security; he was one of two princes to enter Eton in 1995. The other, Prince Narajan, youngest son of King Bivendra Bir Bikram Shah Deva of Nepal, became a friend and William was deeply disturbed at the news of his death, along with his ruling father and five other relatives, in the Himalayan kingdom in June 2001.

In his first year, William would be known as an 'F-tit' which is 'Etonese' for 'squirt' with the 'F' indicating the school block inhabited by all first-year students. His adjustment to life at Eton was perfectly smooth, helped in no small part in that he already knew several faces. 'Freddie' Windsor, son of Prince and Princess Michael of Kent, was an upperclassman while his Ludgrove friends, Johnny Richards and Andrew Charlton, would share the same House. He would also become close to Nicholas Knatchbull, the grandson of the late Lord Mountbatten and a distant cousin.

William was immensely proud of his F-tit status and, as the first year progressed, made a conscious effort to fit in with his fellow pupils. Unfortunately, boys being teenage boys, not all were so welcoming and saw a

confrontation with the future king as something of a challenge. Indeed, he had only been at Eton four months when pupils were issued with a stern reminder that throwing snowballs near the school was strictly forbidden after William had been set upon and had his clothes filled with snow. A gang of boys from his year reportedly rounded on the Prince and bombarded him, stuffing the snow down the front and back of his jumper. One pupil was quoted as saying: "We thought it was awful fun. There weren't any rules about throwing snow, so it seemed perfectly alright."

William suffered from his inevitable and unique status on the sports field; a star inside centre at rugby, he was often selected to represent the first team, but found himself battered black and blue by players from opposing schools who were often hugely enthusiastic to tackle the future king. Parents, who followed visiting teams, would regularly pack the touchlines armed with cameras, waiting for their sons to land a crunching tackle on the Prince. Despite security worries, William would also insist on turning out for the rugby team at away fixtures, although this had to be abandoned when it was discovered that his clothes and name tapes were starting to disappear while he was out on the field of play!

There was no denying that William was suffering a form of victimisation, but not once did he complain to his peers; in fact he took every challenge in his stride and even turned out for the rugby on one occasion with a heavily strapped thumb, such was his desire to carry on playing. He also received great encouragement on the sports field at the time from a friend of his mother, England rugby captain Will Carling, who invited William and Harry to join an England rugby training session. The tuition obviously paid dividends as William's Eton coach and Canadian international, Gareth Rees, paid him the compliment: "William is just great," he said. "He's a competent inside centre and is coming on very well indeed in our rugby coaching." Asked whether he could become the 'king' of rugby, Rees responded: "To me the king has always been Barry John!"

His enthusiasm and never-say-die attitude on the sports field won him the respect of his team-mates. As captain of the school swimming team – he was Eton's fastest swimmer for ten years – and with his desire to try out canoeing, water polo and judo, William was regarded as a true all-rounder. His love of sport also extended to the racetrack. Although too young to get behind the wheel himself, he would often ride off-road motorbikes at Balmoral and had a real fascination with speed. He was a serious fan of Formula 1 and, with three times Formula 1 World Champion Jackie Stewart as a close family friend, was able to gain a real insight into the world of F1 when, in 1992, he accompanied him to the British Grand Prix at Silverstone. During the early morning practice session he met British racing driver Nigel Mansell and climbed into the cockpit of his race-ready Williams Renault. On this occasion William was all smiles for the cameras – especially when Mansell, the future Formula 1 World Champion, handed over one of his famous red-peaked caps.

... but found himself battered black and blue by players from opposing schools who were often hugely enthusiastic to tackle the future king.

William's emphatic progress at Eton was a source of considerable delight to his parents and also his grandmother, Her Majesty the Queen, who was gratified to see him evolve from 'Billy the Basher' the tearaway youngster, into a polite, engaging young man. With Windsor Castle's close proximity, William would be a Sunday afternoon visitor whenever the Queen was in residency and it was during these intimate meetings that she would help prepare her grandson for his future role. They would often meet at 4.00pm in the Oak Drawing Room for tea, where they would discuss William's progress at school and his life outside the classroom. These occasions also provided William with the opportunity to discover the workings of a modern monarchy and see for himself the famous 'boxes' – the red boxes contain details of the Queen's forthcoming engagements and the blue boxes hold documents from the Home Office, keeping Her Majesty informed of governmental affairs.

The Queen was particularly delighted when, in July 1999, William was appointed as one of only twelve senior prefects at the school and sent him a hand-written note of congratulations. His newly attained status meant he could now wear a multicoloured waistcoat and plain grey trousers, instead of the pinstripe numbers, plus extra privileges such as extended free time and a radio in his room. However, his grandmother would not necessarily have been so amused by a bizarre initiation, known at Eton as the 'de-bagging' ceremony, which William was forced to endure. Prefects, due to leave the school that year, shouted and stamped their feet before bursting into William's room. There, they whipped off the future king's pinstripe trousers and disposed of them in the nearest bin – never to be worn again. The Prince's underwear may well have been on show for a few short minutes, but at least he was spared the ordeal of being thrown into a bath of cold baked beans, another tradition apparently not uncommon at England's best-known public school.

That William was happy to participate in such boisterous antics was another example of his willingness to fit in and become 'one of the lads'. This was never more evident than at the school's Fourth of June celebrations in 1997 (Eton's 'Speech Day'), when he invited Tiggy Legge-Bourke as his guest rather than his parents. William had decided that their presence, along with the inevitable media interest, might spoil the other families' enjoyment of the occasion, a decision which both Charles and Diana respected. His mother, however, took deep offence at his choice of guest. Relations between Diana and Tiggy were, by this stage, extremely frosty after photographs were published of Tiggy cuddling Harry outside Sandringham Church.

The princes and Tiggy Legge-Bourke arrive at North Queensferry station for a stay at Balmoral, Easter 1996.

Prince William's Confirmation took place on a warm spring day at St George's Chapel, Windsor, on 9 March 1997. His Confirmation, to the church of which he will one day become Supreme Governor, was conducted according to the Book of Common Prayer by the Bishop of London, the Rt Rev Richard Chartres. This was a departure from the usual royal practice of inviting the Archbishop of Canterbury, in this case Dr George Carey, to confirm the monarch's closest relations. It was reported that the Prince of Wales was unhappy with Dr Carey's preference for modern evangelical forms of worship, although St James's Palace denied that any such considerations had influenced the decision. Those present at the service also included Gerald Barber, headmaster of Ludgrove, and Alan Fisher, a former royal butler. Among the notable absentees was the Duke of Edinburgh, who was on a foreign tour. Charles and Diana both arrived and left for the service in the same car with their two sons and the atmosphere throughout the day was said to be extremely buoyant and relaxed.

'THE KING'S COLLEGE OF OUR LADY OF ETON BESIDE WINDSOR' WAS FOUNDED IN 1440 BY Henry VI to supply scholars for King's College, Cambridge, which he founded a year later. It was intended to be part of a large foundation to include a community of secular priests, ten of whom were Fellows, a pilgrimage church, and an almshouse. Provision was made for 70 King's Scholars (known as 'Collegers') to receive free education while a small number of 'Oppidans' (who lived in the town) would pay for their education.

Henry supplied Eton with a substantial income from land, and a huge collection of holy relics, among which were fragments of what were believed to be the True Cross and the Crown of Thorns. He took a close personal interest in the building which meant frequent changes to the plans. In 1448 the partially constructed church was demolished to make way for another, far grander church. The accommodation for the school along the north side of School Yard was completed in 1443 together with a single classroom below (Lower School) and a large dormitory (Long Chamber) above; College Hall, used for dining by priests, headmaster and scholars, was in use by 1450. Cloister Court, which provided residential accommodation for priests and Fellows, was finished about the same time.

Progress on the new church was, however, interrupted when the Lancastrian Henry VI was deposed in 1461 by the rival Yorkist claimant, Edward IV. Parliament annulled all grants of lands made by the Lancastrians: all the College's lands and possessions were transferred to St George's, Windsor. It is claimed that Edward's mistress, Jane Shore, saved the College by persuading him to restore some of its lands. Although it was saved, the greatly reduced income necessitated the abandonment of the almshouse and a reduction in the number of priests.

At this time, the early 1470s, the pilgrimage church was far from finished: a former Provost of Eton, Bishop Waynflete, came to the rescue and arranged for the choir to be roofed in wood and for the west end to be completed by the addition of the (currently used) Antechapel (1479–82): a fine example of the Perpendicular Gothic style, but only a part of what was to have been England's largest and finest church had Henry's plans been fulfilled.

The third side of School Yard to be completed in its present form was Lupton's Range with Lupton's Tower in the centre. Built in 1520 by Henry Redman (whose work is also to be seen at Hampton Court), Lupton's Range provided extra accommodation for the head of the College, the Provost. The fourth side of School Yard, rebuilt 1689, has as its main feature the Upper School on the first floor, Eton's second and largest classroom. In the middle of School Yard stands a bronze statue by Francis Bird of the Founder in Garter robes, erected in 1719.

Today, Eton College enjoys a reputation that is second to none, having educated so many great men over the centuries. The school has expanded to about 1,280 boys aged 13–18 (the 70 Collegers for whom Henry originally provided, the remainder being Oppidans), admitted by competitive examination. Apart from a large part-time staff, there are 143 masters and a governing body composed of a resident Provost and Vice-Provost together with 10 non-resident lay Fellows (successors from 1869 of the ten priest-Fellows of the original foundation).

Most of the boys are resident in the UK but the school also attracts students from overseas. Almost 20% of the boys receive some form of financial assistance such as scholarships and bursaries.

This is the last frame I ever took of Diana. She was in Bosnia on behalf of her anti-landmine work when we were invited to a photo opportunity at Balmoral. I never saw her alive again. RN

Despite the obstacles, there was an unbreakable bond of love and compassion between mother and son and within weeks, William would join Diana and Harry on their summer vacation to Castel Sainte Terese, Mohamed Al Fayed's villa in St Tropez. The three were a picture of joy and contentment as they relaxed on Al Fayed's yacht, with William demonstrating his considerable nerve and skill when he dived 35 ft – higher than an Olympic high board – into the clear blue Mediterranean sea. Although the Queen was reported to be less than happy with this behaviour, Diana simply wanted to give her boys a good time. It would also be the last time all three would share such an intimate moment together.

In the aftermath of the royal separation, Charles, perhaps ill-advisedly, cooperated with Jonathan Dimbleby, the notable broadcaster, who was writing a substantial biography of the Prince. And, in what was to prove a watershed moment which defined for many years to come how the public would view the heir to the throne, gave Dimbleby a 'warts-and-all' television interview, shown on the BBC in June 1994. Shock waves reverberated around the world as Charles admitted to committing adultery with Camilla Parker Bowles throughout his marriage to Diana. Not unnaturally, the confession was believed to have caused both grief and embarrassment to William, but even before the dust had settled, he would be hurt further as Diana sought her revenge in an interview for the BBC's *Panorama* programme broadcast the following November.

In a candid, 55-minute interview with correspondent Martin Bashir, the Princess discussed her husband's affair, her subsequent depression, eating disorders and her belief that there was a Palace conspiracy orchestrated against her. Yet for William, more damning was the admission that she, too, had been unfaithful with former Life Guards officer James Hewitt. "Yes, I adored him … But I was very let down," said Diana. For William, his mother's admission was an act of betrayal. Although he had never met Camilla Parker Bowles, he regarded James Hewitt as a long-standing, close, personal friend.

Hewitt first came into four-year-old William's life when he encouraged Diana to develop her equestrian skills around the grounds of Windsor Great Park. He would also help William with his ponies and the three formed an immediate close friendship. As the months and years went by, Hewitt became a regular visitor to Kensington Palace; a sporting, enthusiastic associate for both princes in the absence of their father, and a more intimate companion for their mother.

While Diana was naturally upset at the impact of the revelations on both her sons, the interview somehow transformed her life. To some extent it set her free from the shackles of her failed royal marriage and she would now be seen by many as a beautiful, liberated woman in her own right.

On 28 August 1996, divorce proceedings were finalised and although she lost her HRH status, she would be known as Diana, Princess of Wales. Now under even greater public scrutiny, and with William's blessing, she decided to cut back on her official engagements. The number of charities she actively supported was reduced to just six.

Her divorce and subsequent retirement from many aspects of public life left the Princess with more time and liberty; she would be less inclined to keep her relationships under wraps from now on. But Diana had underestimated the almost obsessive fascination that the press and public would continue to have in her life. There was intense press interest in the Princess and concern was growing in the royal household that Diana's behaviour was becoming increasingly wilful. Shortly after Diana and the boys' holiday at Harrods owner Mohamed Al Fayed's villa in St Tropez in July 1997, a British newspaper announced, in what they claimed was a world exclusive, that Diana had found a new love, naming Al Fayed's son Dodi. She and Dodi were photographed in late July on Fayed's yacht as they sailed along the Cote d'Azur. It was a relationship that would ultimately have tragic consequences. Diana's last public appearance was in Bosnia in mid-August, where she continued her anti-landmine work, while the British press was invited to Balmoral for an informal photo opportunity of Charles, William and Harry.

It was proving to be a difficult summer for William; there was little doubt that he was torn, trying to remain loyal to both parents and splitting his time between them equally. He had enjoyed the glamorous lifestyle holidaying with his mother in St Tropez, but he also loved the outdoor life – hunting, shooting, fishing and riding – that made up his time at Balmoral, where he stayed throughout August with Harry, his father and the Queen and the Duke of Edinburgh.

The last holiday together. William and Diana in St Tropez just a few weeks before she died.

Death of a Princess

As William turned in exhausted on the night of Saturday, 30 August 1997, following a day's fishing on the banks of the nearby River Dee, he did so knowing that he would be reunited with his mother the following week. Having been apart from Diana for the best part of a month, both William and Harry were excited at the prospect of their return to Kensington Palace and had packed their belongings in readiness. They would, indeed, still make their eventual return to London but the events of the next few hours would make it a sombre, heartbreaking and totally devastating affair.

With the royal household sound asleep, Charles was woken at 1.00am with the news that Diana had been severely injured in a car accident in Paris. She had been enjoying an evening at the Paris Ritz with Dodi Fayed but, aware that a group of photographers had gathered in the plaza outside, the couple had decided to leave through a back entrance to the hotel and into a waiting Mercedes, driven by Al Fayed employee, Henri Paul.

Unfortunately, the couple's attempts to escape the pursuing press proved futile as a fleet of motorbikes and mopeds hounded them through the streets of the French capital, and as the chase grew ever more dangerous, the sleek, powerful black Mercedes disappeared into the Pont d'Alma at precisely 11.30pm – with heartbreaking consequences.

Charles was made aware by the Queen's deputy private secretary, Sir Robin Janvrin, that both Dodi and the chauffeur Paul had been killed in the crash and although Diana had been seriously injured, her condition was not thought to be life-threatening. There was no reason at this stage to upset the princes unnecessarily and Charles remained in his study to await further news. A report was received that the Princess had suffered a broken arm and concussion, alleviating fears and raising hopes within Balmoral. But within two hours relief turned to total devastation. Charles received another call; Diana had died on the operating table of the Pitie-Salpetriere hospital in Paris.

Deeply shocked, Charles had the dreadful task of telling his sons the appalling news. Very little has been said about these painful hours, but it is believed that Charles let his sons sleep until morning before breaking the news to them, after which he and the boys spent much of the morning with their grandparents, who tried to comfort them as best they could. They

would also be joined by Tiggy Legge-Bourke, the one person to whom they could pour out their hearts and tears and who would be able to provide much-needed comforting hugs.

But even the sudden devastating loss of their mother did not prevent adherence to royal duty. Just hours after receiving the news, the young princes, clearly upset and in shock, attended Sunday service at the nearby Crathie Church. It was tradition that whenever the royal family were in residence at Balmoral, they would attend the service and on the 31 August 1997, it would be no different.

As they drew up in one of three black Rolls-Royce limousines, the boys sat either side of their father and as they came into view of the assembled media and local well-wishers, they bowed their heads, looking very pale. Wearing grey suits and black ties, in public they remained dignified and calm. Incredibly, no mention was made of Diana during the service.

On their return to Balmoral an hour or so later, plans had to be made for Diana's final journey home. Putting aside all the bitterness of his divorce, Charles took a pivotal role in the proceedings, deciding he would travel to France to accompany Diana's body back to the United Kingdom. It was as if death had finally brought the warring Waleses together; one small crumb of comfort for William on this most traumatic of days. Although he was keen to go to France, the rule about flying with his father was uppermost in everyone's minds and so Charles flew to Paris with Lady Jane Fellowes and Lady Sarah McCorquodale, Diana's sisters. William, although disappointed, remained behind to provide care and support for his younger brother. In moments of crisis, William has always been there for Harry, all normal sibling rivalries forgotten.

As the events of the week unfolded, William and Harry would remain at Balmoral to gather their thoughts and learn more about the events surrounding their mother's death, mainly through television and radio.

Following an autopsy in a private mortuary in Fulham, Diana's body was transferred to the Chapel Royal at St James's Palace, where crowds had flocked in their hundreds of thousands to lay flowers, sign the books of condolence and, quite simply, pay their respects. As the momentum of national grief gathered pace, London almost came to a standstill; Buckingham Palace, The Mall and Kensington Palace, in particular, became vast seas of floral tributes.

The first public appearance of the princes outside the gates of Balmoral, five days after the death of Diana, Princess of Wales.

Yet as the acres of flowers, cards and mementoes continued to grow, the silence from Balmoral began to speak volumes. There was no message from the Queen, no lowering of the royal standard at Buckingham Palace and no word of how the week's events had taken their toll on the young princes. A nationwide, and to some extent media-led, feeling of resentment began to be directed towards Buckingham Palace The increasingly widespread anger at the apparent insensitivity of the royal household to the grief felt by the nation was deepening with every passing hour – there were even calls for the Queen to abdicate in favour of her grieving grandson.

There was little doubt that the royal family had underestimated the deep affection many people felt for Diana. Charles's own efforts were not enough – it was time for the whole royal family to acknowledge the grief felt by the nation. Regardless of her divorce from Charles, and arguably the rest of the royal family, Diana had been the 'People's Princess' and, after all, was the mother of the future king.

The young princes did not appear in public until the following Thursday when, again dressed in sombre suits and black ties, they greeted well-wishers at the gates of Balmoral. While Harry, still visibly upset, remained close to his father's side, William showed poise and dignity as he crouched down to read the vast array of messages on the bouquets and cuddly toys that had slowly built up throughout the week. They then prepared for their return to London, where the princes would complete their journey at Westminster Abbey, to bring to an end the most difficult, heart-rending and mournful week of their young lives.

The following day, the Queen returned to London and finally made her long-overdue address to the nation from Buckingham Palace. She explained that the royal family had remained at Balmoral to help the young princes come to terms with their devastating loss. It is likely that she would have also instructed the boys in the procedures for the forthcoming funeral. Although barely teenagers and deeply upset by the loss of their beloved mother, William and Harry were

nevertheless young royals; they were expected to maintain a dignified presence in the face of the huge outpourings of grief from not only the British public but from people all over the world.

All eyes were on the boys as they accompanied their father, at their own request, on a walkabout at Kensington Palace and they did, indeed, display a courage that moved many of the people present to tears. At this moment, there was, however, no doubting that they were their mother's sons. William again took a lead role, reaching out, touching and even managing the faintest of smiles as he accepted more flowers, tributes and words of comfort from the crowds who had assembled at the gates of the home that held so many happy and lasting memories.

It was then on to St James's Palace where Diana and her boys would be reunited for the very last time. As they approached the black and gold Palace gates and observed more floral tributes – some five feet deep in places – the boys were visibly distressed and almost overwhelmed by the enormity of the week's events, yet they held their emotions in check. To cries of "William, Harry, we love you", William would glance up in that way so reminiscent of his mother and smile shyly before offering a hand and a polite: "Thank you so much for coming."

He then followed his father and Harry into the Palace for their very private moment. The day's events had proved to be a defining moment in William's life. For so long the focus of so much attention, he had only appeared in public to appease the demands of the press. But this situation was unique; this was William appearing on his terms, to give something back to his people. This was not stage-managed – this was the real William – and those who walked away from St James's Palace that night were left in no doubt that among the many achievements in her short life, Diana's greatest legacy would be this young boy who had the character, warmth and compassion he would need for his role as future king in the 21st century. She could be paid no greater honour.

"We fully respect the heritage into which they have both been born, and will always respect and encourage them in their royal role. But we, like you, recognise the need for them to experience as many different aspects of life as possible, to arm them spiritually and emotionally for the years ahead. I know you would have expected nothing less from us."
From the funeral oration by the ninth Earl Spencer.

The following morning at precisely 10.25am, William and Harry waited outside the gates of St James's Palace to accompany their mother on her final journey. Keen that the funeral should not be too staid and sombre, William took a leading role in the preparations. He wanted the occasion to be a celebration of his mother's life; among the 2,000 mourners inside Westminster Abbey were guests from the world of music, film and fashion as well as representatives from the countless charities with which the Princess had been associated.

Both William and Harry made it clear that they wished to remain by their mother's side for the procession. There were concerns that it would be a walk too far for two boys who had endured so much during the past seven days, but, just as they had insisted, they accompanied Charles, the Duke of Edinburgh and Diana's brother, Earl Spencer, on the route to Westminster Abbey. It would be the longest 35 minutes of their young lives.

As the cortège passed through the eerily quiet streets of London, broken only by the sobs of the estimated 1.5 million people who had lined the route, all eyes remained focused on the boys. It was not a journey they had ever envisaged or, indeed, had time to prepare for, but both fell into step with the Welsh Guards who accompanied Diana's body. It was hard for Harry, dwarfed by his elders, to keep up with the pace, but he managed it admirably, while William looked totally oblivious to everyone around him. His eyes remained fixed to the ground, with only his blond hair moving gently in the late summer breeze.

Down The Mall, under Horseguard's Arch, past Downing Street and the Houses of Parliament, the cortège reached the Abbey as its bells finally fell silent. Harry, close to tears, glanced up at the coffin that was surrounded by white tulips, roses and petals – one for each of Diana's 36 years – but William continued to gaze at the ground, hiding his emotions from the sobbing crowd and estimated worldwide television audience of 2.5 billion.

As they entered the Abbey, the strains of I Vow To Thee My Country – Diana's favourite hymn – filled the air. The boys maintained their composure; Harry now courageously kept his eyes on the coffin, placed high on its catafalque, while William clearly struggled to take in the full tragic irreversibility of the moment. He kept his head bowed or covered his face with his hand – just as he had done on a Spanish beach when he was a boy.

But it was the moving words of Candle in the Wind, written specially for the occasion, that proved too much, too unbearable. As Elton John, a long-time friend of Diana's, took to the piano to pay his own personal tribute to 'England's Rose', Harry buried his face in his hands and quietly sobbed. William also cried as Elton John, straining to contain his own emotions, sang his plangent and utterly appropriate composition to a vast audience. The Prince of Wales gave the first of many sidelong glances of support but for a few moments, the boys were left to grieve in the most natural of ways.

Earl Spencer concluded the funeral service with a strident eulogy, attacking the press and also, in a direct reference to the royal family stated: "She needed no royal title to continue to generate her particular brand of magic … She would

As the cortège passed through the eerily quiet streets of London, broken only by the sobs of the estimated 1.5 million people who had lined the route, all eyes remained focused on the boys.

Sandringham, Christmas 1997 and William and Harry collect armfuls of gifts as they leave church where prayers were offered for the life of Diana.

want us today to pledge ourselves to protecting her beloved boys, William and Harry, from a similar fate … I pledge that we, your blood family, will do all we can to continue the imaginative way in which you were steering these two exceptional young men so that their souls are not simply immersed by duty and tradition but can sing openly as you planned."

His speech was followed by an extraordinary round of rapturous applause both inside and outside the Abbey. Although, understandably, the Queen and her immediate family didn't join in the applause, William and Harry quietly clapped their uncle and many felt that Diana, with her deep dislike of endless royal protocol, would have looked down on her boys with a radiant and sympathetic smile.

If Diana had lived, there is little doubt she would have remained under the intense glare of the media spotlight and maintained the same love–hate relationship with the press; but then she would still have been able to offer her unique blend of warmth and affection to those with whom she came into contact. But she had gone now. The 'Queen of Hearts' was no longer able to weave her undoubted spell. For many people there now existed a need for a substitute Diana. With his uncanny resemblance to his mother, both in looks and mannerisms, William could expect to assume that mantle whether he wanted it or not.

There is every hope that he will be happy to continue his mother's legacy. Like the rest of the royal family he had underestimated the place his mother held in the hearts of the nation, and it wasn't until he witnessed the outpouring of grief at first hand did he begin to appreciate the deep respect and love she had generated in her all-too-short lifetime.

William now saw it as his duty to not only fulfil the expectations of the royal family, but while respectful of his position as future heir to the throne, to continue absorbing the lessons his mother had taught him. He would not become a sheltered, restricted royal; he would live in the real world where pop music, fast cars and motorbikes, trips to the cinema and going to rugby and football matches would become a normal part of his life. It is what his mother would have wanted.

Following a private funeral at Althorp, attended by Diana's immediate family, the young princes travelled back to Highgrove with their father, where they would again be met by Tiggy Legge-Bourke. Although the grieving would continue, the day after the funeral, Sunday 7 September 1997, would act as a watershed in William's life. It was time to look to the future, to attempt to get life back onto a more normal footing, even though he would never again be greeted by his beloved mother with a smile or a hug.

William immersed himself in life at Eton, returning to his studies within a week of Diana's funeral. Although initially he found it hard to be parted from Harry (who had returned to Ludgrove), and his father, he once more rejoined the banter and day-to-day challenges of life at school. And at Eton he was shielded, to a great extent, from the outside world.

With all the anger that had arisen following the initial disclosures about the circumstances of Diana's death, William's relationship with the media was, understandably, at its lowest ebb and he was determined there would be no intrusion into his academic life. His public engagements that year were kept to an absolute minimum and, although he made a brief appearance at the premiere of *Spiceworld* – the Spice Girls were William's favourite pop group at the time – he maintained his distance from the both the public and the press.

The first Christmas since Diana's death was fast approaching, which promised to be a difficult and poignant time for the boys still missing their mother. As usual the festive period was spent at Sandringham, where Christmas Day prayers were offered for the life of Diana.

Also present at Sandringham that Christmas were Princess Anne's children, William and Harry's cousins Peter and Zara Phillips. Almost five years his senior, Peter had become a firm friend who in no small measure helped William through the first difficult months after the loss of Diana. Like William, he is a keen sportsman and he is believed to have been responsible for encouraging the Prince's love of rugby, swimming and horse riding. Educated at Gordonstoun, Peter was studying for a sports science degree at Exeter University at the time. Sport was always a regular topic of conversation between William and Peter and, whenever possible, Peter provided swimming and rugby coaching. When William helped Eton to a triathlon relay victory in Wales that academic year, it was reported that Peter had coached his cousin prior to the event.

Peter's sister, Zara, also developed a close friendship with William following Diana's death. Just over a year apart in age (Zara was born in May 1981) they have a lot in common and, in the years to come, would been seen together at polo – a passion they both share.

It was Zara who was at William's side when they appeared outside Clarence House for the 98th birthday celebrations for the Queen Mother. As the Queen Mother and her guests posed at the entrance gates, to the sound of Happy Birthday played by the Welsh Guards, William's growing physical stature was increasingly evident. At Diana's funeral, William's height was equal to his father but now, at 6ft 2in, the 16-year-old stood head and shoulders above his immediate family members. During his sabbatical from public life, a physical transformation had taken place; in place of the boy with the cherubic smile was a tall, handsome, eligible young man. His elegant, regular-featured appearance caused many teenage hearts to beat a little faster and teen magazines were delighted to have a new pin-up. The magazine *Smash Hits* printed 'We Love Wills' stickers. "After Diana's death it seemed the whole world was saying that William must be sheltered from the media," said the magazine's editor, Gavin Reeve. "Now everybody, including his own family, seems to want him to be a sex symbol. He must feel like a rock star on tour."

The great grandchildren gather at Clarence House on 4 August 1998 to celebrate the Queen Mother's 98th birthday.

For the first time in Britain, royalty had become hip. Prince William had become the epitome of cool – joining popstars like Boyzone and Robbie Williams – and, according to sources at Eton, he received more than one thousand Valentine cards that February. His newly attained star status was never more apparent than on a trip to Canada in March 1998, when the world experienced 'Willsmania' for the first time.

Despite the obvious growing interest in William as a pin-up, it is fair to say that nobody looking forward to the royal tour to Canada expected Charles, William and Harry's arrival in Vancouver to be anything but a routine and somewhat tame affair. This seemed to be the case until the party arrived at their base, the Waterfront Centre Hotel, where they were completely thrown off their guard by the frenzied reaction of the welcoming party. A crowd of young girls, teenagers and women of all ages greeted William's appearance with screams, roses and home-made banners declaring: 'William, it's me you've been looking for.' There were further yells of "I love you" as the atmosphere reached fever pitch. Still lacking his mother's skill in handling this type of situation, William looked decidedly uncomfortable.

Obviously embarrassed at being the object of desire for so many girls, William lowered his head and walked sheepishly into the hotel. The crowd's disappointment was palpable. Concerned that his son's behaviour might be misinterpreted as another example of royal stuffiness rather than the shyness it undoubtedly was, Charles immediately offered his own wave and a smile but, not surprisingly, the response from the throng of thwarted young women in the crowd was fairly muted!

There can be little doubt that Charles and William had a long talk that evening, especially as there was every indication that the scenes would be repeated in the coming days. William, at 15, was clearly in need of advice about dealing with the enthusiastic, and predominantly female, crowds. But this was not to be a phenomenon unique to Canada; as the young, good-looking, eligible future King of England, William would continue to be an alluring figure to females the world over.

Above: Still showing signs of teenage nerves, William arrives at Vancouver's Pacific Space Center where a noisy and largely female crowd wait impatiently.

The following morning, what should have been a private trip to Vancouver's Pacific Space Center became a very public affair as more than two hundred girls had managed to track the royal party down. William was subjected to the kind of adulation usually reserved for pop or movie stars. This time he rewarded his admirers with smiles, but his nervous fiddling of his tie suggested that he was still feeling acutely uncomfortable. As the fans waited patiently outside, William and Harry were shown round the complex by 22-year-old Jennifer Nathan. "Every teenage girl in Vancouver is jealous of me," she said. "When I was told I would be showing them around, I was really nervous but now I know I am the luckiest girl in the country."

William and Harry helped to launch a rocket and played complex computer games, but the highlight of the two-hour visit was the virtual reality space mission, which had both boys in fits of laughter. While they were inside the Center, the screams from outside were very audible, but were a mere prelude to the noise generated by the near hysterical crowd that later greeted the boys when they visited Burnaby South Secondary School. There were cries of "William, William, William" and some girls had worked themselves into such a frenzy that they were crying openly as the Prince disappeared into a mass of welcoming arms. The tears, the screams, the wailing simply intensified as he began his walkabout, greeting as many people as his protection officers would allow. With a handshake and a smile, he went about his duty with a greater air of confidence, quite a contrast to the timid Prince seen on his arrival in Canada. William was learning fast!

Prince Harry almost disappeared under a mountain of flowers as girls threw daffodils in William's general direction, while royal aides were drowned under a deluge of cuddly toys, balloons and Canadian flags.

There was little doubt that the tour had been, so far, a complete success; on one level it had announced William's arrival as a glamorous figure for a new generation, while on another it demonstrated the clear bond of love and friendship between Charles and his two sons. This was never more evident than on the next leg of the tour during a visit to a heritage centre on the Vancouver waterfront. Charles had to deliver an important speech about a local scheme to protect areas of the Pacific coastline from further development, but found it increasingly difficult to make himself heard above the noise of hundreds of schoolgirls all shouting for William. By way of appreciation Charles was

In June 1996 Diana had travelled to Rome as guest of the fashion designer Krizia whose shows she would be attending that evening. Diana left Rome airport at high speed while we headed straight for our hotel which was situated at the top of the Spanish steps. I'd just checked in when I heard a growing roar coming from the foot of the steps. Within minutes a crowd of what must have been two thousand had gathered. Without even seeing Diana, we all knew that she must have been the reason for the sudden appearance of the crowd. It became clear that she was having coffee in one of the many small cafés. I couldn't get anywhere near so I took this shot from the top of the steps. It shows just what an extraordinary magnetism Diana had, and no matter where she was in the world, she would always attract a huge following. The question now is whether Prince William will have to cope with such enormous fame. RN

presented with two Team Canada bomber jackets for his sons, plus two 'poor boy' caps, the uniform of the country's Winter Olympic team. Rather than expose his sons to another over-excited audience, it had been decided that Charles would accept the gifts on the boys' behalf. However, deviating from the script and in an impromptu response to the enthusiasm of the Canadian welcome, he encouraged his boys to join him on stage. As they came forward, with their now mountainous collection of cuddly toys and flowers, William continued to steal the show. Slipping off his suit jacket, he put on his new bomber jacket and cap – with the peak at the back – and, in true gangsta rap style, twirled round and gave a roll of his wrist and shoulders. The crowd went absolutely wild. William had acted quite spontaneously, a young man growing in self-confidence all the time. A more fun loving, confident and amusing William was revealed rather than the shy and reserved youth often seen at the more formal prearranged photocalls.

The buoyant mood was infectious and Charles, too, found himself trying on a 'poor boy' cap, showing that despite his reported dislike of having to don unusual gifts of clothing and headgear for the cameras, he was on the same wavelength as his sons.

The royal party then took to the serenity of the slopes above the nearby exclusive resort of Whistler. But there was to be no escaping the dozens of adoring girls who followed in hot pursuit. One group had travelled overnight on a coach, including 14-year-old Jessica Toews who had paid £29 for a lift pass to reach the royals high up in the Canadian Rockies. She explained her infatuation to the assembled press: "He's rich, he's gorgeous and he's a Prince. What more do you need?" Not much, evidently. Diana's successor as the royal star had been found, some reports suggesting that William had become the royal family's saviour.

The very public show of warmth and affection between Charles and his sons at the heritage centre was the clearest indication yet seen that a bond of love and easy friendship between Charles, William and Harry had grown that much stronger since Diana's death. Friends close to Charles had always suggested that

he found it easy to show tenderness towards the boys, but preferred to share his more intimate moments in private. However, Charles now seemed prepared to demonstrate his love for his sons in a public way.

In turn, with a careful balancing act no longer necessary, William was free to demonstrate his natural, loving feelings towards his father. Later that year he was spotted on the tarmac at Heathrow Airport giving his father a farewell kiss – a public show of affection not seen prior to August 1997 – before flying in separate aircraft to Greece for their summer holiday on board *Alexander*, the yacht owned by the late billionaire John Latsis.

The 16-year-old Prince had matured tremendously in 12 short months. Although still regarded by the public as a shy young man, there was little to indicate what really made him tick when out of sight of the cameras. While anxious to preserve William's privacy, the Palace was fully aware of the legitimate public interest in the future king. On the eve of his 16th birthday, William agreed to answer a series of written questions submitted to him by the Press Association.

He maintained a diplomatic silence on many of the questions asked, but was candid on a number of topics. He admitted that he was not always comfortable in the public eye, but disclosed that having sat the last of his 12 GCSEs at Eton, he was set to study A levels in geography, biology and the history of art, giving himself the widest possible choice of options for a future university course. He stated that he enjoyed life at Eton, particularly the college uniform of tailcoat and striped trousers, while his credibility was only slightly dented after admitting to a liking for 'techno' as well as classical music. With garage music and hip-hop at the cutting edge of teen culture at the time, some thought William's love of the harder-sounding techno was indicative of a taste several years behind the times. He stood out further from the average 16-year-old by not owning his own computer – his biggest regret. William admitted to liking fast food, reading action-adventure books and wanted to go on an African safari. Demonstrating a still painful wound, he added that he felt his world had fallen apart when his mother died.

His yachting holiday to Greece over, William withdrew to Balmoral, where the first anniversary of Diana's death was marked. The public's grief at the loss of the Princess was renewed on the anniversary and Kensington Palace was again adorned with floral tributes, but for William, the time had come to let his mother rest in peace. A rare personal appeal was issued on behalf of both boys asking for the public commemoration and grieving to be brought to an end. They acknowledged that public sympathy at the time of their mother's death had greatly comforted them but the Princess herself would have wanted people to now move on. The princes were doing exactly that and, at precisely the time the statement was read out by St James's Palace spokeswoman Sandy Henney, Harry and his father were arriving at Manor House, Eton, to be greeted by Dr Gailey and his wife.

In an oak-panelled room, Harry sat down before the open book, picked up a cheap ballpoint pen and prepared to write his name. "Make sure you sign it in the right place," said Charles, remembering that William had entered his name on the wrong line. "Oh, shut up!" responded Harry in his good-natured yet boisterous way.

William was naturally delighted to have his young brother at the same school. His presence and the benefit of the agreement reached by the press and St James's Palace that they would not intrude on the princes' lives at Eton, meant that William's academic performance was now extremely impressive. He would end the school year passing eight of his GCSEs at grade A and two at grade B.

William would also become the first future king to take on 'alternative employment'. In March 1999, he spent three days of work experience at the London auction house, Christie's – the firm responsible for selling Diana's dresses and raising £2,000,000 for charity. Organised by Dr Gailey, the idea was ensure that the Prince was kept in touch with the real world by introducing him to the daily 9-to-5 routine of work from which so far he had been sheltered. His position dictates that he will never experience this way of life in reality, but he intended to fulfil all the wishes of his 'employer' and even walked to work from St James's

Sandringham, Christmas 1998. Since his mother's death, all the Christmas gifts seem to have been reserved for William.

Palace, just like the thousands of other commuters working in nearby offices and shops. Apart from his protection officer pacing his every step, William fitted perfectly the image of the office junior. Wearing a suit and tie, he arrived promptly before 9.00am where he was introduced to the staff. A guided tour of the premises followed and, like every other 17-year-old, he was introduced to the basics of office junior life: filing, photocopying and even making the tea.

It was still Tiggy Legge-Bourke who remained the boys' closest female confidante and ally. With her outgoing and adventurous nature, in the difficult period following their mother's death she had invariably managed to lift their spirits. At Charles's request Tiggy arranged as many social distractions as their diaries would permit, including a trip on safari.

Ever since Charles and Harry had returned from a trip to South Africa in November 1997, their enthusiastic tales of the glorious wildlife had filled William with a real desire to follow in their footsteps, as he had revealed on the eve of his 16th birthday. For ten days that March his dream would come true as he, Tiggy and his brother travelled through two of southern Africa's great nature reserves, the Moremi, home to millions of birds, and the vast Okavango Delta with its lagoons, islands and countless species of wildlife.

William's wish for a real African adventure was realised as they lived under the stars, navigated the waterways in canoes and observed the elephants, giraffes, antelopes and zebras from their Range Rovers. Charles, so used to the creature comforts in life, chose to opt out on this occasion, but played his part by picking up the estimated £20,000 bill for the trip.

Such was William's determination to be cut off from the outside world that, although his two protection officers were permitted to take a satellite phone with them, not once did either he or Harry feel the need to call their father. In fact, the public had absolutely no idea that the trip had even taken place until the boys returned home to spend Easter with their father at Birkhall, the Queen Mother's home on the Balmoral estate. "We want the public to know that we were working with the press to protect the boys' privacy", announced St James's Palace, "and that the Prince of Wales is extremely grateful." The media's decision to respect the princes' privacy was the clearest indication yet that a common ground had been found between Fleet Street and the Palace. It was an uneasy truce, but with public sympathy still strongly favouring William and Harry, any publication that overstepped the mark knew that a backlash would be inevitable. For the first time in a long time the royals were calling the shots.

His first major solo engagement, as a godparent to Prince Konstantine Alexios, the grandson of the former King Constantine of Greece, was further evidence of William's transition to manhood. Again, he looked more at ease than usual as he stood smiling on the steps of the Greek cathedral of St Sophia in Bayswater, West London, next to the baby's parents, Crown Prince and Princess Pavlos. For the photographers there would be no opportunity for William to be pictured holding the infant as his left arm was heavily strapped in a sling – the result of another injury on the rugby pitch.

As the child lived in New York, his new responsibility as godfather was unlikely to prove too onerous a task. Even King Constantine conceded: "It does not require too much from him – just a phone call once a year." The Crown Prince, himself a godson of the Prince of Wales, went further, saying "Prince William, together with other cousins of mine, has been chosen primarily for the reason that they are from the younger generation of our extended family. I think William is a very good upstanding young man who will be able to help my son when he reaches his age."

William continued to spread his wings. Immersion in school life had helped him come to terms with the loss of his mother and his excellent exam results had given him renewed vigour and confidence. Later that summer William could be found in a marquee-studded Windsor Great Park at the Cartier International polo tournament, surrounded by beautiful people and, more especially, beautiful young women.

Despite his still tender years, William's ripening maturing was obvious. His casual dress usually consisted of sweaters, cords and trainers, but on this occasion the young Prince dressed stylishly and appropriately. Wearing the latest wrap-round shades, blazer and open shirt, he conversed confidently with his table guests. Although the free-flowing champagne was strictly off limits, he looked remarkably relaxed, showing none of the reticence that his legion of female admirers usually engendered.

It is almost certain that William's appearance that afternoon and subsequent column inches in the press would not have entirely pleased St James's Palace, but there was little doubt that the Prince was beginning to find his place in society. William will, of course, be a star in the social firmament around which much of the smart set will revolve in the years to come, and at the Cartier International polo tournament he looked far removed from the teenager who stole so many hearts in Canada the previous year.

His driving test would prove equally effortless. Accustomed to driving around the private grounds of Highgrove, William cruised through the examination in the Wiltshire town of Chippenham, cracking jokes along the way. "It was a faultless display," said Driving Standards Agency chief examiner Robin Cummins. "I felt under no pressure to pass the Prince, although I did think this is one I'd like to get through." As it turned out, there was no question of failure. "At the start I asked him: 'Are you feeling ready for the test?' and he said 'It's now or never'. He was very chatty and relaxed, just like any other 17-year-old youth who has had excellent driving instruction, and on one occasion when a white van came out in front of him, he said, 'They are all out today' … When I told him he had passed, he seemed delighted. His bodyguard got out of the car to allow me to give William the result in private. Then we removed the L-plates and I drove him home to Highgrove. I asked if he had got a car of his own yet. He said 'Yes, but I have not seen it. My father bought it second-hand'."

The date and location of the test had had to be kept top secret because the make and registration of the car he was learning to drive – a silver Ford Focus –

Just before William took his driving test, the press were invited to Highgrove for a photocall – aimed, I would imagine, at curbing any further attempts to track the Prince around the roads of Gloucestershire. Highgrove itself came as a pleasant surprise – in fact this was the first time any of us had been officially invited to the Prince of Wales' residency. As we parked up for the prompt 9.00am start our names were checked off a list. I was struck by the wonderful gardens, but sadly there was little time for a guided tour of the stunning grounds. Once I'd unloaded my cameras from the car, we were ushered into a roped-off area in front of the main entrance and then, all of a sudden, the Prince of Wales and Prince Harry emerged. Almost immediately William approached from the left in a modest Ford Focus before joining his father and brother for a brief chat with reporters. Ten minutes later, we were heading back to the M4 – the job completed. RN had already been made public during a photocall prior to the test. With the press lined up at Highgrove, William had driven sedately into view, managed to brake without hitting a bank of TV cameramen, then got out of the car to join Harry and his father. The object of the exercise was to diffuse newspaper and public interest in William the motorist, but questions about the Highway Code were strictly off limits. Indeed, William remained quiet throughout the morning, leaving his father to talk up his performances behind the wheel. "He's doing very well," said Charles.

William did, however, continue his lessons for sometime after passing his test, taking further tuition from his instructor, Sgt Chris Gilbert of the Metropolitan Police Driving School as part of the 'Pass Plus' scheme. Under this initiative, new drivers are given extra lessons in skills not covered by the regular test such as motorway and night driving. In return, William would have his insurance premium – for the VW Golf his father had bought him – cut by 10 per cent.

The Prince also received tuition in specialist driving skills that are taught to royal and diplomatic chauffeurs and he would prove to be a careful and conscientious driver. Within weeks of passing his test, William grabbed the headlines when he leapt into action with his brother to help two men whose car had broken down. The princes were on a night out with Tiggy Legge-Bourke, who was driving the Range Rover, when they saw Simon Thompson and his friend, policeman Stephen James, having problems with their BMW near Sloane Square in central London. It might have been easier to ignore the situation – as had the countless other drivers who passed the stricken pair – but together with his brother and friend, William van Cutsem, they pushed the car into a nearby driveway. "I couldn't believe it," said computer salesman Thompson. "I was steering and the future King of England and his brother were helping to push my car. When the car was parked, they hopped back into their vehicle and drove off. It was an almost surreal experience but showed that the boys are, indeed, like many other lads their age."

Certainly this was the impression that William appeared keen to give; true he was beginning to enjoy the privilege and trappings that are part and parcel of being a member of the royal family, but he would also derive much pleasure from the social side of student life, which invariably meant a trip to the pub.

Alcohol would not play a part, but William certainly had a enthusiasm for karaoke. During a geography field trip to County Durham, the Prince approached the owner of the Crossways Hotel in Thornley to ask if he and his friends could challenge the locals to a North versus South karaoke competition. In a keenly fought battle, he and three classmates gave a sterling rendition of the Village People hit YMCA while the locals responded with Elvis Presley and Tony Bennett. "It was a really excellent night," said hotel owner John Hudson. "We had had our normal karaoke night on the Wednesday, which had been attended by some of the boys from Eton, and they asked if we could have a second night on Thursday. William and his friends took centre stage for one of the songs and really belted out their song. He really got into it, with all the

"I couldn't believe it," said computer salesman Thompson. "I was steering and the future King of England and his brother were helping to push my car."

hands movements, and he was just one of the crowd, a very natural and polite person. When the Prince left on Saturday morning, he came to me, shook my hand and said 'Thanks for a very pleasant stay'. It was a special moment."

Eton is known for its robust social scene and the College has its own pub, The Tap, in which senior boys are allowed to drink small amounts of beer under the supervision of their Masters – a far cry from Charles's schooldays at Gordonstoun when, in 1963, he was reported to have asked if he could have a cherry brandy to warm himself up after a sailing trip.

Charles was beginning to realise that his son – if and when he should he become king – would not necessarily adopt the style of the monarchy of the past or, indeed, the present. William had proved himself to be a young man in touch with the people. With a little encouragement from Tiggy, Charles responded by ensuring that his sons would be surrounded by as much warmth and comfort as he could possibly provide. Highgrove was now the boys' main refuge from their academic studies and Charles installed computers, the latest hi-fi equipment and video games.

With his father's blessing, William even set up a disco in the cellar for Charles's 50th birthday bash. It is understood that originally both boys had wanted to celebrate this important milestone at a fashionable central London nightspot, but Charles insisted on entertaining his guests in Highgrove's banqueting suite. An adjoining disco proved to be the ideal compromise. The party was also significant in that Camilla Parker Bowles would share the responsibility for making the arrangements for the party and would have to agree matters with the boys.

Highgrove House, in Gloucestershire, was built between 1796 and 1798 and was bought for the Prince of Wales by the Duchy of Cornwall in 1980. The Duchy's main purpose, since the 14th century, has been to provide an income, independent of the monarch, for the heir apparent and the house was purchased from MP Maurice Macmillan, son of former Prime Minister Harold Macmillan.

Charles took up residency shortly after his marriage to Diana in 1981 and immediately went about improving its appearance by replacing the solid parapet with an open balustrade, surmounted with urns. The house itself is a neo-classical, stone-built property, with four reception rooms and six principal bedrooms, but the overriding feature of the 37-acre estate is the spectacular gardens, born from a run-down and exposed area around the house and now regarded as one of the Prince's proudest achievements.

With the help of the Marchioness of Salisbury, a life-long gardener, Charles proceeded to create a rose garden, the redevelopment of a kitchen garden and a stunning 'veritable carpet of colour' that greets visitors along the driveway to the house. A garden terrace has also been created on the west side of the house and each year, Charles chooses a new project to further enhance the floral elegance of the estate. In 2001, his gardening skill and achievements reached new heights when he was shortlisted in the 'best garden' category at the Chelsea Flower Show, for his Islamic Carpet Garden design, which was inspired by the Middle Eastern rugs on display at Highgrove.

William's appearance at the Air Assault Brigade display at RAF Wattisham in 1999 was significant in so far as it was his first official appearance at such an event and further evidence of his interest in the armed forces. He had just been awarded the Sword of Honour at Eton, given to the best all-round cadet at the end of his first year as a cadet, and he looked on with real enthusiasm as a host of military hardware and personnel came into view – on the ground and also from above – courtesy of a display of RAF Harrier jets. Although Charles was the official guest, it was leaked to the press 24 hours before the event that both his sons would also be present, and all eyes focused on William. In the week that followed, there was intense media debate about whether, once he had completed his education, the young Prince would join the armed forces. The speculation only intensified when part of his gap year was spent with the Welsh Guards in the jungles of Belize. Although his future plans remain firmly under wraps, there is a growing consensus that he will, indeed, join the regiment of Welsh Guards after he finishes his degree at St Andrews. RN

An initially somewhat frosty relationship had begun to thaw. William, in particular, had seen so much internal bickering and strife in his young life that he saw no reason to prolong the unease by refusing to accommodate Camilla's presence. With Charles and Camilla making their first 'coming out' appearance on the steps of the London Ritz earlier in the year, William accepted that she was very much a part of his father's life and responded accordingly. In fact, William and Camilla having successfully collaborated in organising Charles's party, would, later in the year, be seen together on holiday for the first time. It was a far cry from their first meeting when William unexpectedly walked in on his father and Camilla at St James's Palace, having dropped in to change his clothes. William and Camilla spoke informally together while drinks were served. She was said to have been 'extremely nervous' and 'greatly relieved' at the outcome.

Camilla and her children, Tom and Laura, joined Charles and the boys aboard the *Alexander* for a cruise around the Aegean. She was invited at William's insistence; a significant step as just seven years earlier, Charles, Diana and the boys had taken the very same trip, their last together as a family.

As the millennium drew to a close and with William's 18th birthday fast approaching, speculation mounted about his future and, more immediately, his choice of university. Following a display by the 16 Air Assault Brigade and 12 Mechanised Brigade at RAF Wattisham, Suffolk in September 1999, which William watched with real fascination, reports were widespread that he might choose a career in the armed forces. He looked on in excited anticipation as the Harrier jets screeched overhead and paid great attention as the helicopters, Land Rovers and elite paratroopers came into view; a subsequent talk on the weaponry and vehicles seemed to fuel his curiosity. The Prince had also visited the Special Air Service at its Hereford base, resulting in suggestions that a career with the SAS was imminent.

At Eton, sixth-formers, as part of the curriculum, are offered a choice between voluntary community service and joining the Cadets Corps. William chose the latter and was awarded the Eton Sword of Honour – the school's highest accolade for a first-year cadet – presented after consideration by the officers of the Corps and a training officer from the Honourable Royal Artillery Company.

His coming of age was accompanied by the release of a fuller interview, a portfolio of pictures and television footage, intended to put paid to some of the endless conjecture. In order to avoid an out-and-out media scrum, the Prince allowed one photographer and one television cameraman into Eton. The picture that emerged was that of a modern young man – a sportsman, pin-up and, rather surprisingly, a budding chef! One intriguing piece of footage saw William cooking chicken paella; cooking was his preferred choice of 'general studies' and it was not unusual for him to prepare a three-course lunch under the guidance of teacher, Jane Lowther. "I'm just following orders" William explained as he went through the recipe step by step with his friend Ned. "It usually works out even though Ned and I are the worst cooks in the world." With those words, disaster struck as he swamped the pan when pouring in the chicken stock. There was a brief moment of panic until the Prince gathered his composure, showing his leadership skills by ordering his friend to: "Do something – quickly!" Nevertheless, between them they did manage to produce a respectable paella. Other clips showed William working at a computer and striding the college grounds in his Union Jack waistcoat, the privilege of the Eton prefect. He was also seen playing football, water polo and swimming.

Royal Ascot is the world's most famous horse race meeting, steeped in a history that dates back to 1711, when Queen Anne saw the potential for 'horses to gallop at full stretch'. By August of that year Her Majesty's Plate was run and the seeds had been sewn for a magnificent sporting and social occasion, which to this day embraces tradition, pageantry and style. More than 300,000 people visit the racecourse annually, which is a stone's throw from Windsor Castle, and, on any given day of the five-day meeting, at least one member of the royal family household will be in attendance.

Perhaps the member of the royal family most closely associated with horse racing was the late Queen Mother and in another tradition the pupils from nearby Eton would serve tea to Her Majesty and her guests on the Wednesday of Royal Ascot week, in the Royal Pavilion at Windsor Great Park, as a number of polo matches were played out in front of her on Smith's Lawn. This occasion, in June 1999, was particularly interesting as several members of the royal family were in attendance, including Princes Charles and Andrew, who looked more like actors from the hit TV show *The Sopranos* in their sunglasses.

The University of East Anglia emerged as his first choice and he confirmed that he had applied to read history of art and that he planned to take a gap year before taking up his place at university. William expressed his dislike of being in the media spotlight and commenting on the alleged advances of pop princess Britney Spears remarked: "There's been a lot of nonsense put about by PR companies ... I don't like being exploited in this way but as I get older it's increasingly hard to prevent ... I like to keep my private life private." He also revealed that he would not assume full royal duties until he had finished his education,

although he might accompany his father on some royal engagements. While he was studying, he would prefer to be known as William Wales rather than the full HRH title, which would normally be adopted at 18. He stated that he did not want people to bow, curtsy or call him 'Sir'. He refused to be drawn on his future career, saying that he had yet to make up his mind. With his Eton days coming to a close, he admitted that he would miss his friends and Dr Gailey — likewise the uniform of waistcoats and wing collars!

William walked out of Eton for the final time on 29 June 2000, bringing to an end one of the happiest chapters in his life. Although it had been clouded by the death of his mother, he had been able to study and develop in an atmosphere of relative normality. With Dr Gailey's care and guidance, he had excelled in both the classroom and on the sports field, but probably the achievement of which he was most proud was his election to the Eton Society, or Pop, the small group of prefects who are elected by their peers and whose badge is the choice of a colourful waistcoat. William, on his election, sported a Union Jack model and occasionally one in blue with large white polka dots — the more garish the better. Pop was originally a 19th-century school-debating society that met in Mrs Hatton's lollipop shop which then stood on a site next to Manor House, where the Prince lived at Eton. Modern-day members do not have quite the same authority as their predecessors; while they can impose small fines to keep the other boys in order, the beating of the buttocks and heads down toilets are strictly outlawed! This must have been of some relief to William, who always behaved with the greatest decorum at school.

Private visits to Westminster Abbey and the House of Commons maintained the quiet preparation for his role as the future king. William reached 18 a very rounded and accomplished individual, a son of whom Charles was justly proud – as indeed Diana would have been had she lived to see her son come of age.

Gap Year

William's preference to study for his degree in the history of art at the University of East Anglia was seen as an unconventional choice. The intervention of Dr Andrew Gailey would see the Prince head north of the border to the University of St Andrews, based at St Andrews, a small town in Fife as well known for its golf as its academic institute. Founded in 1411, St Andrews has the biggest art history department in Britain after the Courtauld Institute.

The fourth choice of public school students (behind the universities of Oxford, Cambridge and Durham), it is the only university in Scotland where undergraduates wear gowns and it has a lively social scene. Former students include politician Alex Salmond, author Fay Weldon and, more, importantly Dr Gailey, William's mentor and housemaster.

William travelled to St Andrews for a tour of the campus and met Peter Humfrey, professor of the School of Art History, who told him that he would be expected to visit galleries, museums, present dissertations to tutorial groups, and to graduate with 'visual literacy: the ability to assess images of all kinds critically and perceptively'. Not only did the university impress William, also it was argued that his choice would be good for St Andrews and for Scotland. Although there were the inevitable worries about security issues – with just six thousand undergraduates, compared to some eighteen thousand at Edinburgh – it would be much easier to protect the Prince within the confines of the small medieval town, which has just three main streets. Additionally, both Balmoral and the home of his grandmother Frances Shand-Kydd were relatively close by. If he wanted something more lively, then he would also be in the right place – St Andrews boasts twenty-two pubs, more per capita than any other town in Scotland! Known as 'St Randy's', its reputation for outlandish parties is legendary. "We like to work hard and play hard," said Marcus Booth, president of the Students' Association at the time. "Every night there is something happening, lots of dinners, lots of balls."

William made his choice official once his A level results had been published. Although he was in the jungles of Belize at the time at the start of his gap year, his results were conveyed to him by Dr Gailey, who congratulated him on achieving a grade A for geography, B for history of art and C for biology. He also received a congratulatory email from his father. These results, allied to his successful GCSE results, gave William the best set of marks achieved by any

member of the royal family since being allowed to sit public examinations some 33 years earlier, when Charles obtained a C in French and in history at A level after passing five O levels (although he failed at maths). Diana did not take any A levels and once famously remarked that she could not answer a Trivial Pursuit question because she was 'as thick as a plank'.

William's planned gap year would allow the university a full 14 months to prepare for his arrival and straight away plans were drawn up to ensure his entry would be as smooth as possible. Safety was of paramount importance; the university's Principal, Dr Brian Lang, gave up his baronial mansion close to the town's famous golf course, so that the School of Art History could be housed under one roof rather than spread over five separate buildings. The high walls and trees surrounding the house would add to William's privacy, while the Fife Constabulary were also called upon to increase the security around the university walls. Disturbingly, the Royal Protection Squad found electronic surveillance equipment during a sweep of the campus, but it was the only breach of security discovered during a careful search of the buildings.

William's impending arrival at the university also led to a 44 per cent rise in applications, which in turn created its own problems. A greater intake of students would lead to an increased chance of stories about the Prince making their way into the press. This was a major concern to William who, quite naturally, wanted to enjoy all that university life had to offer without fear of being endlessly discussed and exposed in the press. Dr Lang made it clear to the entire student body that he would take a dim view of anyone found guilty of passing information onto the media or encouraging the presence of the press. Interestingly, William has now reached the halfway point in his degree course and there has been very little intrusion into his life at St Andrews. The respect his position commands, the high personal regard in which he is held by his fellow students and the media's adherence to the agreement that they would leave the Prince alone, have meant his university years have hardly made the pages of the newspapers at all.

While Dr Lang and his colleagues were spending the year fine-tuning the arrangements for the Prince's arrival, impending university life was the last thing on William's mind as he embarked on his gap year. To celebrate the end of his A levels and to recharge his batteries, he spent some time with his brother and friends at Rock, the small resort on the northern coast of Cornwall, a favoured haunt for many public school teenagers. He spent the long days in his rubber suit on a surfboard, playing tennis or fishing. Evenings were spent either at the Oystercatcher bar or around the campfire, listening to music which, given plenty of free-flowing beer, was often accompanied by dancing to the latest house and garage music.

But just idling his time away is not part of William's make-up; he is an adventurous and ambitious individual who wants to experience all that life has to offer. It was his intention that his 12-month sabbatical should be an opportunity to broaden his horizons and test himself physically. He greased down his surfboard, washed the sand out of his hair and quit these shores, in secrecy, for the tiny Central American country of Belize to train with a unit of the Welsh Guards.

To help William's transition from Eton schoolboy to rugged adventurer, former Welsh Guards captain Mark Dyer would accompany William throughout his gap year. The Prince would certainly need Dyer's knowledge of jungle warfare for his first tentative steps in Belize. Out of telephone contact with the outside world, William would train with 140 Welsh Guards as they trekked through dense and steamy undergrowth housing scorpions, snakes, tarantulas and wild boar. With temperatures that rarely fall below 35°C, William would battle the constant threat of malaria and, more worryingly, leishmaniasis, a parasitic disease transmitted by the bite of some species of sand flies which, if not treated properly, has a 40 per cent mortality rate. Accompanied by Dyer, five members of the Royal Protection Squad and two SAS soldiers, he took part in a series of exercises with the Guards, codenamed Native Trail. His first task was to build his 'home' – a palm-leaf shelter, known as a basha, which looks like a four-poster bed, 3ft off the ground and made of logs and bamboo shoots. He would sleep to the sound of the jungle and the mosquitoes trying to penetrate his netting, a far cry from the creature comforts of Highgrove!

The survival programme then began in earnest. William was given a lecture on the four basics of jungle survival: shelter, water, food, and warmth. Armed with a machete, water purification tablets, malaria pills and a sachet meal in case of an emergency, he set off into the unknown. Determined to learn how to be self-sufficient, he assisted instructors in slaughtering a pig, gutting a chicken and creating a culinary delight known as termite stew (echoes of his paella-making days at Eton!). He ate the dish without suffering any untoward consequences, but was clearly more at home with the weaponry at his disposal and the mock attack on 'an enemy base' in which blanks were fired from SA80 machine guns.

"William will make a good soldier," declared Corporal Claud Martinez of the Belize Defence Force. "He has the physical structure and mental strength. He was surrounded by men firing machine guns but he still looked at ease. I never saw a moment of panic in his face." However, there must have been considerable relief within the royal household when William returned home in one piece, having completed stage one of his gap year with considerable success. On his return, he joined his father at Balmoral for more shooting, but this time with a more familiar target – grouse. This was the first opportunity for Charles to congratulate his son in person on his recent A level successes. Although generally Charles did not approve of motorbikes, as a reward for all he had achieved Charles presented William (who had passed his basic motorbike test that April) with a new 125cc motorbike with the proviso that it was to be used exclusively on the estates of Highgrove and Balmoral.

In September, William went on a snorkelling expedition to the tiny volcanic island of Rodriguez in the Indian Ocean as part of the Royal Geographical

"William will make a good soldier," declared Corporal Claud Martinez of the Belize Defence Force. "He has the physical structure and mental strength. He was surrounded by men firing machine guns but he still looked at ease. I never saw a moment of panic in his face."

Society's marine observation programme. He spent much of his time involved in the scientific investigation of ocean currents, the introduction of conservation areas to the island and the education of fishermen, who were intent on the environmentally destructive form of catch explosives rather than the more labour-intensive method of casting and hauling. The trip was in direct contrast to Belize; William's spare time was spent in Dyer's company and only the laughter of their fishing, motorbike and scuba-diving excursions broke the peace and tranquillity of the surroundings. One of the most enduring images from the trip was of William, dressed in only his beach attire, showing the locals how to form a rugby scrum and score a try – no mean task when the people spoke only a Creole patois! To William, who was coming increasingly under close public scrutiny, Rodriguez must have felt like utopia. His accommodation was little more than a corrugated iron-roofed lodge at the end of a potholed dirt track, where he cut a truly anonymous figure for the entire four weeks of his stay. Even the estate's housekeeper, Michelette Eduard, who would regularly serve him a breakfast of ham, eggs, cheese and beans, was completely unaware of his identity. "We had no idea who he was," she said. "It was only after people started talking about him being on the island that I realised who I had been looking after."

As soon as he returned home, William was made all too aware of the tiresome intrusions that come with being a future king. So far there had only been sketchy reports of the Prince's gap year activities and there was, not unnaturally, a growing interest in his exploits, so in an effort to appease the media and public's interest, and in return for continued privacy on further expeditions, a rare press conference was arranged at Highgrove. Dressed informally in a Burberry sweater, jeans and trainers (in direct contrast to his father who wore a conservative suit and brown shoes), William explained that the next stage of his gap year would take him to Chile for a 10-week environmental expedition with Raleigh International. He spoke enthusiastically about the forthcoming trip and about his visits to Rodriguez and Belize, but amidst the smiles a cloud was threatening to overshadow the morning's proceedings.

Patrick Jephson, Princess Diana's former private secretary, had published a damning book. He had suggested, in no uncertain terms, that Diana possessed a manipulative and hysterical personality, and was, ultimately, a scheming liar. His exposé, which was being serialised by the *Sunday Times* at the time, had clearly distressed William. When the inevitable questions arose, he responded: "Of course Harry and I are both quite upset about it – that our mother's trust has been betrayed and that, even now, she is still being exploited." Charles stood firmly by his son's side ready to offer support and solidarity. This was the first occasion William had responded publicly to any attack on his mother, and he seemed glad of the opportunity to make his feelings known. Returning to the main themes of the morning, this was William's press call and he clearly enjoyed being in charge. He explained he needed to do something constructive in his year off. The expedition to Chile would offer the opportunity for him to meet a wide range of people, while at the same time helping those in the remotest areas of the

Opposite: For only the second time the press had been invited to Highgrove. It was William's press call to explain his forthcoming 10-week expedition to Chile and dampen the not unreasonable media interest in the gap year, which so far had been somewhat under-reported. When we arrived we photographers were told that when our (brief) time with William had ended, the press conference would be for reporters and television and radio journalists only. The decision to exclude us was not explained, but as Patrick Jephson's damning book on Princess Diana's life had just been published and serialised in a national newspaper that week, maybe the presence of flashing cameras, that would automatically fire off as soon as the inevitable line of questioning came up, was regarded as being too intrusive. As it was, we spent five minutes taking our shots of William, who looked every bit the handsome young prince in his casual Burberry sweater, jeans and trainers. Then he moved on to take his position for the main conference and once he was in place, I took this picture by turning 90 degrees from my restricted position, and managed to get this great shot of the assembled press eagerly focused on their subject. From where I was standing I certainly couldn't hear what was being said and I'm not even sure I should have been taking the picture at all, but it was instinctive and remains a favourite because it shows clearly the fascination the future king holds for the press. RN

country. "Some friends of mine said how nice the Chileans were, so I thought why not see how it is," he said. "I chose Chile because I had never been to South America before and I also wanted to go somewhere colder rather than hotter."

William also explained that he would be joined by 100 other volunteers, aged between 17 and 25, and that he had raised £5,500 towards the trip by organising a sponsored water polo match. Asked whether his father had also provided financial assistance, he grinned and said "He might have helped slightly" to which Charles retorted: "I chip in all the bloody time!" William, who had seen and met many troubled and disadvantaged people with his

mother as a boy, would now find himself travelling and living with a very varied mix of young people, all guests of the Raleigh International organisation.

The first stop-off point was Patagonia at the southernmost tip of the continent, where the chilly conditions and rugged countryside were reminiscent of Balmoral, albeit on a much larger scale. Following a week's induction, the volunteers split into groups and were sent out across the region. William embarked on a kayaking trip which should have taken in the deep ocean fjords of the region and dramatic coastline but which, due to the adverse weather conditions, became instead, first a perilous journey into the unknown and

then a hasty retreat to first base. "The wind whipped up into a storm," he recalled. "The tents were flapping so violently that we thought that we were going to blow away. I had never seen rain like it. It did not stop." For five days, William's party were trapped on a sand bank. He later admitted to it being the most demoralising part of the trip as his days were confined to chopping wood and sitting round a campfire. He said he had felt "very fat" but once the conditions improved, the group made up for lost time by kayaking in pairs and William burnt off the excess calories by playing football with a group of salmon fishermen he had befriended, using their nets as goalposts.

More nights sleeping rough were spent in the Tamago National Reserve, where the group followed the rare huemul deer population, but not until they reached the isolated Pacific coastal village of Tortal, some 950 miles south of Santiago, would William and his companions find shelter at the local nursery school. He entertained the local schoolchildren enormously as he attempted to teach them English, while they in turn tried to help the Prince brush up on his GCSE Spanish. He did, however, run into trouble while trying to explain the 'W' in his own name. Standing before the 10- and 11-year-olds, he wrote his name out on the blackboard. Struggling to think of an animal with the same initial letter, he wrote: 'My name is William. I am a wombat.' But when he tried to draw a picture of the said animal, he looked perplexed. "How do you draw a wombat?" he wondered out loud. He continued to amuse the children by zipping up his fleece over his head – which drew loud applause when the zip got

stuck – and he held hands with the children as he sang the Hokey Cokey and Old MacDonald had a Farm. He also scribbled affectionate messages on the children's books. "One of the great things about Will is him being so natural with the kids," said Team Leader Marie Wright. "He plays games with the kids in the local nursery, he picks them up, chucks them around and runs around like a kid himself."

The trip would, inevitably, have its more mundane moments; erecting walkways between the villagers' homes was constructive and satisfying, but chopping trees and making wooden supports would prove arduous. To help with these tasks William and his group borrowed a stereo and sang in unison to the Tom Jones hit Sex Bomb. Music would, indeed, provide a welcome respite throughout the trip and, with a local radio station just a stone's throw from their HQ, it was going to be too big an opportunity for the Prince to miss. "Hello all you groove jets out there!" announced William as he gave a passable impression of Ali G, much to the amusement of the Radio Tortel DJ.

"This is 'Tortel Love' and we are in the mood for some real grooving here …" William never looked more at ease than when mixing with the locals and the language barrier proved no obstacle as he danced the salsa into the small hours at the Celes Salom nightclub in town and sampled the cuisine at the town's high school. "He loved the jam, he liked it so much he ate it straight off the spoon," said teacher Fresia Vergare. It was an honour for this reclusive community to have their lives touched by royalty, but his fellow volunteers treated him as an equal.

Getting up at 6.15am to prepare breakfast – described as a "a disgusting sludge of lumpy porridge" – washing dishes, cleaning the toilet and sleeping on the floor of their leaky nursery certainly helped break down any initial barriers that existed between William and his less privileged companions. "Marigolds are now officially a fashion item," he proclaimed. "I'm with a group of people I wouldn't normally be with and getting along with them is great fun and educational," he added. "Although I found it difficult at first, because I am a very private person, I learnt to deal with it. There are some real characters in the group who don't hold back any words at all." He experienced at first hand the type of language used by members of the group when he took a shine to Sasha Hashim, a trainee beauty therapist from the Wirral, Merseyside. "The next thing I knew he was trying to pull my girlfriend," recalled Kevin Mullen, a reformed drug addict from Glasgow. "Let's just say that words were exchanged. It was nothing nasty because he and I get on very well. But I don't care if you are the future king – you don't start messing about with other people's girlfriends."

It was a situation the Prince had never really had to confront before, but he handled it with diplomacy and grace. In the company of former drug addicts, the long-term unemployed and youngsters with a history of crime, he built bridges with them all. He became quite close to Mullen despite their lives running on very different tracks. Football proved a common ground and they spent many hours discussing the merits of Aston Villa and Kevin's favourite team, Glasgow Celtic.

This experience of working with and helping the underprivileged fuelled a desire in William to learn more about the lives of ordinary people living near his home at Highgrove. On his return to the United Kingdom, he spent a month working as a labourer at Hill Court Farm, near Tetbury in Gloucestershire, which would involve working a number of backbreaking 12-hour shifts that included milking cows, shifting bales of silage and washing down the parlour floor. He would enjoy the comfort of a drink in the local pub with the other farmhands and the luxury of his own bed (Highgrove was just five minutes away), but he never once ducked his duties and reported promptly at 5.00am each morning. He regarded his time in the company of Rupert Cox, the farm manager, as one of the highlights of his gap year. "I loved working on a farm, before foot and mouth, which is partly why I've got so much sympathy for the farmers who have suffered. I was put in as a hand, was paid, and was just another guy on the farm."

Opposite: "One of the great things about Will is him being so natural with the kids," said Team Leader Marie Wright. "He plays games with the kids in the local nursery, he picks them up, chucks them around and runs around like a kid himself."

It was reported that William earned £4.70 an hour but what was more important to him was being immersed in the countryside and the outdoor environment. It came as no surprise, however, when he announced that he would spend the greater part of his gap year back in Africa, among the game reserves of Kenya and Tanzania. During his three-and-a-half month visit, he would learn about game conservancy and African wildlife. He would marvel at the sight of the rare black and white rhino, antelopes grazing, lions hunting and the herd of elephants that once strayed into his path.

William joined park wardens on a night anti-poaching patrol, travelled bareback on a camel and would spend many days under the tutelage of Ian Craig, whose lodge became a base during the trip. But it wasn't only the wildlife that would attract his attention; other guests at the lodge included three young children who had lost their mother, Loo Mathews, in a car accident in Nairobi that January. Drawing on his own experiences, William would often put a compassionate arm around 8-year-old Justin, Sean, 13, and sister Tanith, 11, during evenings spent around the campfire.

The trip to Africa would also see the Prince court controversy over his liking for hunting. While riding with a group of European farmers known as the 'Kenya Cowboys', William responded to the call 'Ndege' (meaning bird), pointed his 12-bore skywards and fired. Once the applause had died down, it emerged that the Prince had made a mistake. The victim was not the game bird as first thought, but the habada ibis, a protected species in Kenya. Dr Samuel Kanyamibwa, head of the country's World Wildlife Fund (WWF), was forthright in his reaction: "It is not acceptable," he said. "It sets a very unfortunate example. Apart from anything else, firing weapons frightens the other animals." William's actions brought some condemnation back home, but fortunately this was the only adverse publicity from a trip – indeed the whole gap year. A tired, but fit, tanned and extremely happy Prince returned to celebrate his 19th birthday and to prepare to take up his place at the St Andrews University in September.

Members of the Aston Villa Wesleyan Church formed Aston Villa Football Club in 1874 and the team was one of the founders of the Football League in 1888. By this stage they had already won their first trophy, the FA Cup, in 1887 and they dominated the game at the time, winning the championship five times in its first twelve seasons. Most of Aston Villa's history has been spent in the top division, but success was only found in various cup competitions until 1981 when they took their first league championship for more than seventy years. They followed this in 1982 by winning the European Cup, beating Bayern Munich in the final. Villa came close to another league title in 1990 and they again finished second in 1993's inaugural Premier League season.

William has never spoken of his decision to support 'The Villa' ahead of the more successful London clubs of Arsenal and Chelsea or, indeed, the world-famous Manchester United, but it is believed that he began following the club in his early years at Eton. Yet it wasn't a particular player or game that won his affections; by all accounts he had to pull a name out of a hat and then stick to supporting that team. Villa was his choice and he has remained loyal to them ever since.

University Years

With bags packed, security measures carefully rehearsed and trusted pens, brushes and pastels safely stowed away, William embarked on his journey north to St Andrews. He would stay with friends before his first day at St Andrews, but his enthusiasm and anticipation for this next crucial stage in his life was cut short suddenly by the events of 11 September 2001.

After a late night out, William had just arisen as the horror began to unfold. In shocked silence, he sat with his friends as the awful reality of the terrorist attacks on the United States of America began to sink in.

Ten days later, he and his father would visit the American Consulate in Edinburgh to sign the book of condolence. William, looking sombre and thoughtful sat, with his father, at a desk decked with the stars and stripes to pay his tribute to the thousands of people who lost their lives in New York, Washington and Pennsylvania. He pondered for a moment and then, in his distinctive left-handed style, penned the words: 'With deepest sympathy, love from William' before turning to the staff on duty to offer his heartfelt condolences. "I wrote 'with deepest sympathy' because it was a tragic thing that happened in America," he later said. "I wanted to let them know that they are not forgotten and that people do care about them. I just watched the news that morning and sat there stunned for ages. No one said anything. It was such a serious loss of life."

That he chose to make a very public appearance spoke volumes about his intentions to embrace Scotland and its people. He stated that he didn't want to go to an English university "because I have lived there and wanted to get away and try something else". He also pointed out that he would be seeing a lot of Wales in the future but he loved the hills, the mountains and, indeed the spirit of the Scottish people themselves.

William had witnessed at first hand the degree of community spirit operating in even the poorest parts of the country, when, on the same day he had been to the American consulate, he joined his father on a visit to Sighthill, one of the most impoverished housing estates in Glasgow. The purpose of the trip was to discover for himself the extreme contrast between life in the inner city and the tranquillity to which he had become accustomed in the glens surrounding Balmoral.

For a young Prince whose day-to-day life was far removed from that which now stood before him, it could have been a daunting experience; yet as he had demonstrated in Chile, William had by now developed an uncanny knack of

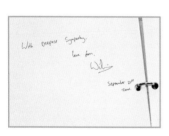

William and his father at the American Consulate in Edinburgh ten days after the traumatic events of September 11th.

fitting in wherever and with whomever he comes into contact. He flirted with pensioners on his arrival at a luncheon club and when 76-year-old Norma Wood suggested that he looked like his father, William retorted: "Oh, don't say that. I can't bear it." He also looked on intently as four young Somalian refugees put on a spectacular break-dancing show; although he declined to participate, he astounded them with his knowledge of garage music by asking 15-year-old Sami Omar "Do you know MC Neat?"

Having dropped in on The Lighthouse, an organisation devoted to helping persistent truants and young offenders, William finished his public day in Scotland with a visit to 'Dancebase', an international dance centre. He approached Lucia Falconer, a Brazilian dancer exotically attired in a silver embroidered costume and asked her to dance for him. She agreed, and produced a Samba show to the delight of both princes. As the spectacular came to a close, William embraced the overawed performer and her partner in a sincere show of appreciation — to a storm of camera flashes! William's openness that day and his willingness to work with the press was something of a pre-emptive strike. He had made himself accessible in the hope that during the four years he would spend studying for his art history degree, he would be accorded the same privacy that he had enjoyed so completely at Eton and throughout his gap year.

FOUNDED IN 1413, ST ANDREWS IS THE OLDEST UNIVERSITY IN SCOTLAND AND THE third oldest in the UK. It was quickly recognised as one of the leading universities of Europe and by the late Middle Ages had three endowed colleges: St Salvator's (North Street) founded in 1450, St Leonard's (now united with St Salvator's; its chapel is off The Pends) founded in 1511 and St Mary's (South Street) founded in 1537.

Bishop James Kennedy, who built St Salvator's collegiate church (1457–60), and his niece Katherine have been remembered since 1849 in an end-of-term student rag known as the Kate Kennedy Pageant.

St Andrews was the first university to enrol women (1862), the first to form a Students' Union and the first to have a marine laboratory (1882). Famous graduates include poets William Dunbar and Sir David Lindsay of the Mount, James Graham, Marquis of Montrose (1612–50), and the inventor of logarithms, John Napier of Merchiston (1550–1617). Its rectors have included Andrew Carnegie, Sir James Barrie and the explorer Fridjof Nansen; one of its principals, Sir David Brewster, invented the kaleidoscope in 1817 and went on to play an important part in the development of photography.

The University also has a strong link with America. Benjamin Franklin was awarded an honorary degree by St Andrews, as was the legendary golfer Bobby Jones 200 years later. Three of the signatories of the 1776 American Declaration of Independence received degrees and the dollar sign was allegedly 'invented' at the University.

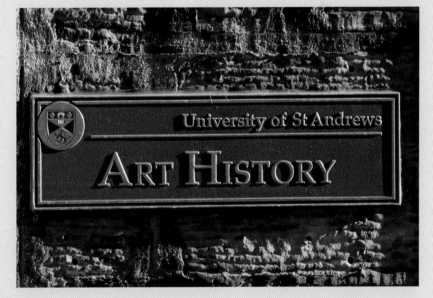

Today, the University encompasses both the sciences and the arts and, physically, it is closely integrated with the town: the modern purpose-built library and many academic schools are located centrally, the growth in physical and mathematical sciences has been accommodated at the North Haugh on the edge of St Andrews, and a modern sports centre with adjacent playing fields and halls of residence are also located in the same area.

St Andrews is relatively small, despite being a 'city', with a population of around 16,000. The University population (staff and students) numbers approximately 6,000. On average, every one in three people in the city will have some connection with the University.

The relationship between a news photographer and his subjects, especially when they are members of the royal family, is complicated by being at times both distant and occasionally complicit. We sometimes need their help and on this particular assignment the Prince demonstrated a considerable degree of media awareness. And in so doing made my life a lot easier than it might otherwise have been.

The whole day had been a little strange and tiring. It was less than two weeks after the shocking destruction of the World Trade Centre and that morning we had watched as William and his father had signed the book of condolence at the American Consulate in Edinburgh. The day was due to finish at a venue called Dancebase and I needed the final pictures of the Prince for the next day's world's newspapers, but somehow a combination of the overall mood – everyone was still feeling a sense of loss after the events in New York – and the cramped and crowded venue meant I wasn't getting anything worthwhile. Then out of the blue William seized the initiative. Spotting these two girls in their Samba costumes he pulled them over and smiling at the now rather amazed press corps put his arms around their shoulders giving us the picture we were all desperate for – actually only a couple of us were quick enough to respond! Five minutes later the picture was on its way to the office and five minutes after that it was all around the globe. RN

Having avoided Freshers' Week, the Prince stated on his arrival that he just wanted to "be an ordinary student" and in his first year he insisted on living at St Salvator's Hall within the university campus. With nearly six thousand other students at the university, six out of ten of whom were from state schools, William would find himself, like every new university student, in a largely unfamiliar environment. His experiences of the past year of mixing with all manner of people would prove extremely helpful, but it is understood that William found the transition particularly difficult.

Although he continued to flourish in the lecture room and again demonstrated his sporting talent by gaining his colours with the university water polo team, it was widely reported that William was wary of fellow students befriending him. He found it difficult to find a social set in whom he could confide with any real confidence. There was even speculation that he was seriously considering a switch to Edinburgh, where several of his old school friends were studying.

Whether William was unsettled in his first year is open to conjecture, but his decision to set up home in a flat by the famous golf links would suggest he had overcome his early problems. As evidence of his renewed enthusiasm he made his first public appearance at a student fashion show at the end of his first year. He turned up to cheer on a friend Kate Middleton, who stunned the audience with her risqué black lace dress over a bandeau bra and black bikini bottoms. Despite the media presence, William took a front row seat. He would also become a leading player in the establishment of a new university social club, made up primarily of old Etonians, and was also said to be frequenting the local

hostelries on a more regular basis – in particular the popular Ma Bells pub – although his second-year timetable would curb many late nights.

With his lectures no longer within walking distance, William is often to be seen racing along on his mountain bike with his bodyguards following close behind. On the surface he looks like an ordinary student, albeit from an extraordinary background. William's timetable for art history this past year has meant rising early for a 9.00am

Already clear is the Prince's ability to put all those he comes into contact with at ease and, with a good deal of charm and self-assurance, comfortably chats to anyone, just like his mother. Although he remains light years away in terms of social standing, he is a person to whom these teenagers at a truancy prevention programme can relate.

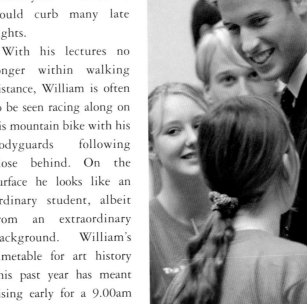

start. Unlike many students, William, as a member of the royal family, is well used to early starts. Once inside, William may seem like any other student, but the scene outside confirms there is royalty in the building. The Royal Protection Squad is on constant patrol in and around the campus and in the adjoining streets of the town centre. After a morning of lectures – and probably an email session or two – it's then back on the bike and home for lunch. After a quick bite, William returns for afternoon practicals, which take place three times a week.

Daytime appearances are a rarity for the Prince. Security reasons aside, the St Andrews system works on a module and credits basis, which means that William has to study more than one subject until third year honours, leaving him precious little spare time. This past year, he has chosen to make up his credits with first year moral philosophy and must attend three further lectures and one tutorial a week.

With a mountain of coursework, it is understandable that William is not often seen on weekday evenings, but his life is not all work and no play. At Ma Bells, on the famous Scores Street, he finds himself among St Andrews' highest social set where the bar, in the basement of the beautiful Golf Hotel, boasts a décor fit for a prince.

Wednesday afternoons are traditionally free periods for St Andrews students and William often spends his free time in the gym. Rugby, football and water polo continue to play a prominent part in his life and he often spends two hours in the pool of the nearby St Leonard's Girls' School to sharpen up his polo skills. Beyond this sketchy outline, little else is known of the Prince's campus life: his friendships, behaviour or, more importantly, how he is progressing with his studies. The press continue to abide by their agreement to allow the Prince a level of privacy unusual for such an important and beguiling figure and his fellow students are well aware that little mercy would be shown by the university authorities if they talk to or in any way encourage the press.

Certainly as the years pass following his mother's death, there appears to be a thawing in relations, and much building of bridges, between St James's Palace and Fleet Street. This was highlighted when William, with his father, appeared at the tenth anniversary party for the Press Complaints Commission (PCC) at Somerset House in February 2001. Dressed in a dark blue suit, blue-striped shirt and polka dot tie, William took centre stage as he thanked the newspaper editors for "not giving me a hard time" at Eton and during his gap year. He also expressed his appreciation for the PCC's continued support and the diligence of their work.

Having left the stage to rapturous applause, William, accompanied by his father, mingled with a host of high-profile celebrities including Joanna Lumley, Carol Vorderman, Donatella Versace and cast members of *Coronation Street*. It had been a new experience for the Prince to be exposed to such a demanding audience, but he had handled it with aplomb. He impressed on the guests that he wanted to be known at 'William' and not 'Sir' and promptly picked out actor John Savident, who plays Fred Elliott in Coronation Street, before adding mischievously, "I recognise you. I watch *EastEnders*."

The Press Complaints Commission is an independent body that deals with complaints about the editorial content of newspapers and magazines. All complaints are investigated under a Code of Practice, which binds all national and regional newspapers and magazines. The Code — drawn up by editors themselves in 1991 — covers the way in which news is gathered and reported. It also provides special protection to particularly vulnerable groups of people such as children, hospital patients and those at risk of discrimination. The challenge for the industry was to show that self regulation could be made to work, and that standards of reporting, which had declined in the 1980s, could be improved. The industry, famously, was 'drinking in the last chance saloon' and it had to demonstrate that it could put its house in order.

The night was also notable for the presence of Camilla Parker Bowles who, in a dark blue cocktail dress with chiffon sleeves, made her first public appearance in the presence of William. Although she maintained a low profile throughout the evening and often lagged some distance behind Charles, her invitation seemed to signify a growing acceptance in royal circles that she is, and will always be, a part of Charles's life.

The loss of the Queen Mother, at the age of 101, on 30 March 2002, while Charles and his sons were still enjoying their skiing holiday in Klosters deeply upset William. He had enjoyed many visits to Birkhall, and his arrival at St Andrews had allowed both William and his great grandmother to meet more regularly, the Prince often joining the Queen Mother for afternoon tea. As had the Queen, the Queen Mother would encourage and advise William, as future heir to the throne, on the role he would have to assume one day, but often she would reveal her less well-known amused and amusing side. "Anything that was meant to be formal and went wrong, she enjoyed," he said in glowing tribute. "She would have a good giggle. She had a young sense of humour and loved a good laugh, even if the joke was about her." He also added that she even tried to invite herself to some of his parties at university – but he resisted her attempts because she would have danced him under the table.

The night before the funeral both William and Harry were in the gallery of Westminster Hall watching their father, Prince Andrew, Prince Edward and Viscount Linley hold a poignant vigil as hundreds of mourners slowly walked past the Queen Mother's coffin. With their eyes lowered, the boys looked on intently as their ashen-faced father stood in a profound state of grief, his hands clasped around the hilt of his sword. Towards the end of the vigil, William and

Harry descended from the gallery and, leading the rest of the royal party, joined the queue of mourners. They waited patiently for their turn to pay their respects, once or twice glancing up at the statues of the Saxon Kings who look down from the walls of the Hall. As they slowly walked past their father both boys looked at him anxiously, before bowing their heads again. They filed respectfully past the coffin before heading outside into the glare of the courtyard. A crowd applauded and shouted "God Bless" as the princes appeared and stood quietly talking to mourners as they too came out into the sunshine.

The next day William and Harry would take part in the Queen Mother's funeral and, as the bells tolled and the gun carriage carrying the coffin with its floral tribute of white lilies, started its short and final journey to Westminster Abbey, it was impossible not to think back to another funeral nearly five years earlier. Although physically now much taller, the boys' dark suits and sombre expressions were a sad reminder of Diana's passing. On this occasion, William did, however, look steadily at the coffin and it was clear that he was offering much emotional support to his visibly upset father, remaining close by his side throughout the service. Looking dignified and every bit the young royal under the most difficult of circumstances was further evidence that William's transition from boyhood to adulthood was now very much complete. Few teenagers can claim to have packed in such a wide range of experiences in such a short time, but they will all prove essential when the Prince one day fulfils his royal destiny.

Grief is etched on the faces of the royal family at the funeral of Her Majesty the Queen Mother. Prince William would recall her impish sense of humour: "Anything that was meant to be formal and went wrong, she enjoyed."

On a happier note, it was a more radiant William who clearly enjoyed many aspects of the Queen's Golden Jubilee celebrations as they reached their climax over the first four days of June 2002.

On the Sunday, he travelled to Swansea with his father and Harry for a special service of thanksgiving at St Mary's Church in the city centre. Although the visit did not attract anything like the hysteria that had met the princes' tour of Canada several years earlier, there were still cries of "William we love you!" as he greeted the 3,000 strong crowd. When they entered the church for the hour-long service, the soccer-mad boys could have been forgiven for letting their minds wander elsewhere as, at the same time some 6,000 miles away in Japan, England's World Cup campaign was kicking off against Sweden. The boys had asked to be kept informed of the score line and as the final uninspiring 1-1 score filtered through from Saitama, the princes no doubt felt, as did much of the country, that this was a worrying and depressing start to England's World Cup campaign. But their spirits were soon lifted as they returned to London to join in the carnival-like atmosphere that was already in full swing, with pomp and colour and ceremony evident throughout the capital.

To an extent, the success of the Jubilee celebrations and the huge public show of affection for the Queen took some commentators by surprise. There had been several years of public antipathy towards the Royal Family after Diana's death, but it was now clear that, for the time being at least, the modern-day public had once again warmed to Her Majesty.

The Queen had attended a classical concert staged within the grounds of Buckingham Palace on the Saturday, and two days later clearly took great delight in a pop concert, featuring Eric Clapton, S Club 7, Paul McCartney, Brian May, The Corrs and Emma Bunton, likewise held in the grounds of Buckingham Palace, which Her Majesty joined rather late. William would be observed clapping vigorously and roaring with laughter as Lenny Henry, Dame Edna Everage and the Kumars injected their own brands of humour into the proceedings.

The final day couldn't have gone any better and William appeared proud and honoured to be a part of such an historic occasion. He waved energetically from the carriage he shared with Prince Harry, the Duke of York and Princess Beatrice as it preceded the gold state coach in which the Queen travelled to the national service of thanksgiving to be held in St Paul's. Magnificent weather greeted the Queen's coach, on only the third ever occasion of its use, as it left Buckingham Palace to the cheers of a crowd so vast that The Mall looked like a sea of red, white and blue and to the sound of a 41-gun salute, one for every minute of the journey to the cathedral.

Later in the day, after the Queen and Duke of Edinburgh had returned up The Mall in an open-topped Range Rover, with hundreds of children waving gold streamers running alongside, the Royal Family watched the Festival of The Mall parade from the royal box on the Queen Victoria Memorial. William and his father, along with Harry, had walked from St James's Palace to their seats, stopping and chatting to the public along the way.

The climax of the day and the Golden Jubilee weekend was the appearance of the Queen and senior members of the royal family on the balcony of Buckingham Palace to watch a flypast which included Concorde and nine RAF Red Arrows jets streaming red, white and blue smoke. The cheers of the crowd were so loud it was difficult to hear the noise of the aircraft.

William was said to be deeply moved by the sight of the estimated one million people who lined the streets of The Mall that evening to greet his grandmother. If it hadn't crossed his mind before, the events of the Golden Jubilee weekend would act as a reminder that the royal family still held a very special place in the hearts of the nation and that one day, a similar turnout could well be lining the streets of the capital to welcome him to the throne of England.

A month later William attended a royal garden party held in the grounds of the Palace of Holyroodhouse in Edinburgh. As he made his way around the grounds, he welcomed many of the four thousand guests and thanked the Scottish people for making him feel so at home during his first year at university. Although the presence of Camilla Parker Bowles attracted some interest, it was William who took centre stage, his 6ft 2in frame and trail of admirers making his progress readily apparent. He made a point of speaking to as many of the representatives from voluntary organisations, charities, community groups and

William acknowledges the cheers of a vast crowd as they watch a thrilling flypast by Concorde from the balcony of Buckingham Palace.

art organisations as time would permit and posed on the steps of the Palace with his father for the handful of invited photographers, an act which drew widespread applause.

Despite his now obvious growing confidence and ease during the limited number of public engagements that the Prince has so far undertaken, the question is will William live up to the expectations that so many hold for him, especially those who argue that he is the best, and quite possibly the last, hope for the British monarch?

On the eve of his 21st birthday, this blue-eyed, blond-haired Prince, with his enviable good looks is clearly not weighed down by either his royal heritage or the prospect of a future life largely given over to duty and public service – immense privilege notwithstanding. He is the compromise of two ultimately ill-matched parents: Diana, who made it her tragically short life's work to ensure her son enjoyed levels of normality and common everyday experiences unique for a future heir to the throne and Charles, who initially subscribed to a view that William's early life would mirror his own in which tradition and duty took precedence over family life.

Charles, at 21, was a mass of hand-wringing uncertainties and has since worn a pained expression of recrimination at what life has thrown at him; William, in contrast, is confident, sure of himself and cannot be blamed for making it clear that he is determined not to surrender his life to an endless schedule of royal duties until his university education is completed – at the very earliest.

He is the product of two very different philosophies, and yet all the signs are that, as Prince William reaches maturity, Charles and Diana together have produced a son of whom any parent would be justly proud.

WILLIAM

HIS LIFE IN PICTURES

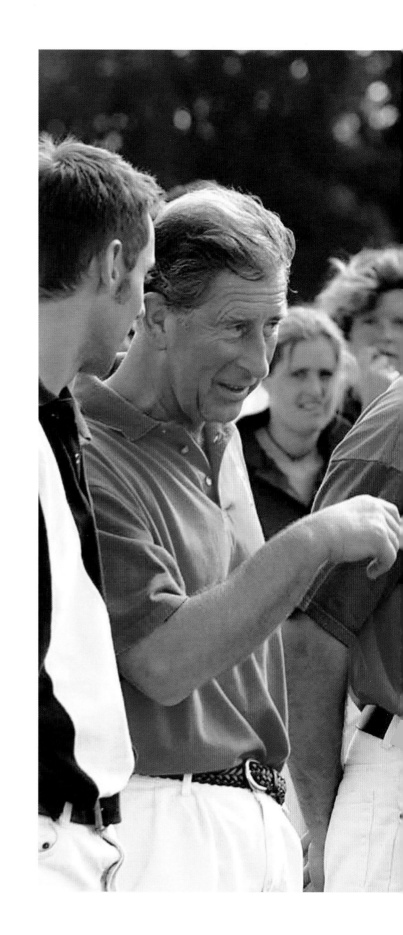

The Prince and Princess of Wales leave hospital
with Prince William 22 June 1982.

Diana plays with William on the banks of
the River Dee, Balmoral 18 August 1986.

Christmas Day church   The old estate fire
service, Sandringham   engine, Sandringham
1987.   3 January 1988.

Walkabout in Cardiff on St David's Day
1 March 1991.

Tug-of-war, Wetherby School sports day
12 June 1990.

Costa del Sol 28 July 1994.

William and Diana play tennis at Ludgrove
1 July 1994.

Wetherby School sports days 1988 and 1989.

Rowing on the Thames whilst at Eton
18 April 1996.

Diana's coffin at St James's Palace
6 September 1997.

'Willsmania' Vancouver, Canada
24 March 1998.

Whistler, Canada
26 March 1998.

William meets the press, Highgrove
29 September 2000.

Gap year, southern Chile
November 2000.

William and Harry hunting with Beaufort Meet,
Gloucestershire 18 January 2001.

Queen Mother's funeral
5 April 2002.

Highgrove
29 September 2000.

Polo club, Cirencester
15 July 2001.

Arriving at Aberdeen Airport 14 March 1986.

Sunday church service, Sandringham
7 December 1986.

William's first day at Mrs Mynor's Nursery
School 24 September 1985.

Guards Club polo, Windsor 23 July 1989.

Christmas Day
church service,
Sandringham 1987.

The old estate fire
engine, Sandringham
3 January 1988.

Diana and William at polo 28 June 1987.

Trooping the Colour 15 June 1985.

At polo, Windsor
17 May 1997.

Sandringham estate 28 December 1989
and 6 January 1990.

Trooping the Colour
16 June 1990.

William and Zara Phillips at the Easter
church service, Windsor 3 April 1988.

Earl Spencer's wedding,
at Althorp
16 September 1989.

Easter, Windsor
March 1989.

Easter, Windsor 19 April 1992.

Holidaying in the Scilly Isles 2 June 1989.

William and Harry ride quad bikes,
Aspen, Colorado 1995.

Diana and William, Nevis, Caribbean
3 January 1993.

Aboard a launch on their way to join the yacht
Alexander, Lefkas, Greece 12 August 1995.

Lodge near the Balmoral estate
11 April 1996.

Cirencester Polo Club,
15 July 2001.

William and Zara play bicycle polo,
Tidworth Polo Club 13 July 2002.

Cirencester Polo Club,
15 July 2001.

Highgrove   Scotland
29 September 2001.   21 September 2001.

Start of Easter skiing holiday, Klosters,
Switzerland 29 March 2002.

William and Harry leave the vigil for
the Queen Mother 8 April 2002.

Thanksgiving service for the Queen Mother,
St Paul's Cathedral 11 July 2000.

Garden at Holyrood   Liverpool 2 April 1982.
House 2 July 2002.

Christmas Day,
Sandringham 2002.

Scotland 21 September 2001.